Eddie Paul's Extreme Chopper Building

Copyright

©2006 Eddie Paul
Published by

kp **krause publications**
An Imprint of F+W Publications

700 East State Street • Iola, WI 54990-0001
715-445-2214 • 888-457-2873

Our toll-free number to place an order or obtain
a free catalog is (800) 258-0929.

Library of Congress Catalog Number: 2006904246

ISBN 13-digit: 978-0-89689-248-4
ISBN 10-digit: 0-89689-248-4

Designed by Jon Stein
Edited by Brian Earnest

Printed in United States of America

Dedication

This work is dedicated to my office manager and friend, Peggy Busick, who unexpectedly passed away as I was completing the manuscript for this book. It is not until a person is gone that you come to realize and truly appreciate how much a part of your life that person was. Not only did Peggy manage her office duties at E.P. Industries, Inc. in her own efficient way, but she was also a total enthusiast of all the work we do. She is survived by her three children and her husband, Bruce, who is also a friend and fellow employee. We will all miss her dearly.

This book is also dedicated to the three people in my life that have made the most impact on me. The first is God, who changed my life and gave me a direction and a reason to set an example of a Christiam in my line of work. The second is my wife, Renee, who God put in my path so many times that I had to marry her to get her to travel in the same direction as I do. Then Renee gave me the third person: our daughter Ariel, who completes the circle, who makes life fun, and who is dedicated to God.

Eddie Paul

Acknowledgments

Special thanks go to Rad and Victor of Boss Hoss, all of the sponsors and manufacturers who participated in the build-up of Chopper One, and to my employees (in no particular order): machine shop foreman Jon Forseth, shop mechanic Bruce Busick, and the rest of the crew consisting of Al Cadena, Jose Camargo, Jeff Tapley, Mario Harders, Rich Bojorquez, and Dave Mansfield for the support as well as the ulcers they have given me.

Very special thanks to:

Brian Hatano, my general manager, who not only helped me with the building of the two bikes in this book but with the photography and writing of my books as well.

Foreword

I met Eddie Paul through a mutual contact at Snap-On Tools so I knew we had at least one thing in common right from the start. As a "car guy," I love to meet other car guys, and Eddie falls into that category at the top of the list. It's not often that a guy can go to a shop today and see the type of customizing that started hot rodding back in the '50s and '60s. Those were the years when I became familiar with names like Winfield, Roth, and Starbird, and the cars that they built helped to build my enthusiasm for high-performance and customizing.

Another thing that Eddie and I have in common is that we're also motorcycle enthusiasts. We both ride bikes as often as we drive our cars and the bikes that we ride have to be as unique and powerful as the cars that we drive. One of my recent acquisitions is a 502-cubic-inch big-block Chevy-powered Boss Hoss, which was delivered straight from the factory to Eddie's shop for a custom pearl blue paint job. While I was there, I got a preview of some of the madness that was taking place. Eddie Paul's well-disguised insanity was clearly evident at every workstation in his shop! The Chopper One build was well underway and every reader of this book will get an over-the-shoulder look at how the whole outrageous project came together. Eddie's pursuit of invention, business and mechanical marvels, along with his total enthusiasm for custom bikes, makes him the ideal person to write a book on building the ultimate chopper.

From one rider to another, I think you'll really enjoy *Eddie Paul's Extreme Chopper Building.*

Jay Leno

Contents

Introduction

Fact: The appeal of choppers has spread like a wildfire from the elite biker crowd to a fast-growing segment of the general population.

While there are many books about building custom motorcycles, or choppers, most are focused on the simple how-to of assembling a "kit" bike. No publication, or bike builder for that matter, has ever entered the realm of building a truly unique big bike, I mean a *really* BIG bike! So, we at Customs by Eddie Paul thought it was time to build the ultimate chopper, and there is nothing larger or more ultimate than the Chevy 350-cubic-inch V-8-powered Boss Hoss motorcycle…with one exception. That's right, we're talking *502 cubic inches of Rat motor on two wheels!* The Chevy big-block-powered Boss Hoss is the latest addition to the awesome V-8 line of musclebikes from the Dyersburg, Tennessee,

motorcycle factory. So, with the help of Victor Vert's California Boss Hoss franchise in Torrance, California, we acquired an "off the shelf" motorcycle outfitted with the ZZ502/502-horsepower aluminum head Gen. VI Chevrolet big-block "crate" engine.

In my shop, nothing in stock form lasts very long, and the Boss Hoss, as radical and jaw-dropping as it is, was promptly stripped to its bare frame as soon as it rolled through the doors. I suppose I could have done a build on a Harley-Davidson platform, but then we would just have another Harley chopper book. My goal here was to create the ultimate chopper, and having a bike with twin-supercharged Rat power (more on the dual blowers later on in the book!) is about as ultimate as it gets. As you'll see and read about in this book, the build principles are basically the same as with

Eddie Paul's Extreme Chopper Building

any other type of bike; it's just that the Boss Hoss parts are a lot bigger and heavier. There's absolutely no doubt in my mind that when this beast was done, it would be the most ground-shaking, window-shattering, mind-blowing chopper ever built!

Extreme builds and fast-paced work are part of everyday life in my shop. But capturing the build-up of Chopper One required us to slow things down considerably in order to photograph the entire process. Although I'm giving you readers a very detailed step-by-step guide to building Chopper One, I don't expect that any one of you will actually venture out and attempt to do anything quite as outrageous as this. But if you're into bikes, or thinking about building a bike, you'll definitely be able to benefit from the wealth of information and tricks of the trade that this book contains. Most of the work that goes into any custom bike is not that difficult to perform if the process is broken down into simple steps. You will gain skill and knowledge as you move from one project to the next, and if you acquire the necessary tools along the way, you'll be as good and capable as a pro builder before you know it.

One thing that you'll notice throughout this book is that I never opt for the easy route of just adding a part to the bike unless absolutely necessary. I will take the time and labor and money for special tools to design a part, build a wooden plug for it and fabricate it out of a flat piece of metal. While this is not the fastest way to build the bike, and certainly not the cheapest or easiest avenue, it is the only way to come up with something truly unique. It's also the best way to demonstrate fabricating techniques and the use of special tools that every builder should know.

This book is not designed to be read from cover to cover, even though you could. *Extreme Chopper Building* is a guide for design, fabrication, mechanics and painting of all things on two wheels; and much of it can be applied to four-wheeled vehicles as well. But all useful things aside, it's sheer entertainment value that I am most hoping to provide. This book is all about the ground-up fabrication of the most awesome chopper ever built! Being a patriotic kind of guy, I fondly refer to this project as the first bike fit for the President (hence the name "Chopper One"). One thing is for sure: the streets will never be the same again once this machine rolls out!

Chapter One

The Secret Weapon— Our Mad Five-Day Thrash To Build The First "Ultimate Chopper"

It's not a bad idea to flex your creative muscles once in a while. Because of the diverse nature of work that we take on in my shop, all of the guys that specialize in custom cars and bikes are not always working on cars and bikes. In fact, it could be several weeks or more between car/bike projects, so to "oil up" the team and mainly just to show everyone that we could do it on a moment's notice, I took on the challenge to build a custom military-themed bike…*in five days!* Not that anyone ever doubted that we could build cool stuff on short notice, but it sure doesn't hurt to pop out a fast custom bike or car every now and then. Tackling a project that would easily take several months in a normal shop and getting it out the door in less than a week is what my crew and I do best.

For those of you who know my wife and me personally, it is no secret that we are flag-waving Americans who voted for George Bush for president. I guess you can say that we are in-your-face Republicans and this is our year. So in light of that, we are expressing our freedom of creative expression by designing the bikes in this book with a patriotic flair. Right before we started the build on Chopper One, Skip Johnson from the *Motor Trend* car show circuit called me one evening and wanted to know if I had any show-worthy customs that could go on tour as a featured vehicle along with all the new cars. In that conversation he stated that the tour would kick off in San Diego, California, home of the nearby Marine base at Camp Pendleton. Since a good percentage of show goers would be from the base, Skip asked if I possibly had anything with a military slant.

I thought about it for a while and called Skip back the next day and said, "How about if we build a custom bike with a military theme based on a Boss Hoss motorcycle?" And then I added, "and I'll build it in only five days!…and produce a DVD/video on the build as well!" Skip agreed and we had a deal. So the "Secret Weapon" concept was born, and having documented the whole five-day build-up with photographs, I'm able to give you a step-by-step look at a custom bike fabrication under one of our extreme deadlines.

All it usually takes for me to become creative is deadline pressure, and many times I create my own pressure just to get the creative juices flowing. I have noticed that I am more creative and productive when a deadline is looming, so when on those rare occasions a deadline does not exist, I convince the crew and myself that we have one, if for no other reason than just to keep things moving. Have you ever noticed that some people with handicaps accomplish more than people with no handicap? Helen Keller, who was sight-, speech- and hearing-impaired, learned to communicate. The famous Greek orator, Demosthenes, overcame a speech defect. Beethoven, in spite of his (late in life) deafness, composed some of the world's most beautiful music. The French novelist, Emile Zola, once got a zero in his final exam in literature. Plato had vision problems, but yet saw what no man had ever seen before, and Albert Einstein flunked math in school.

Resistance builds muscles, handicaps enhance abilities, and deadlines produce results. I love deadlines!

The Secret Weapon—Our Mad Five-Day Thrash To Build The First "Ultimate Chopper"

Jeff Teague is one of the best automotive designers around and happens to be an old friend, so when I decided to do this project he was drafted to make a few renderings for the project.

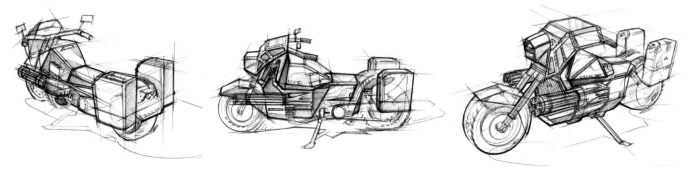

These sketches were made after the fact as we jumped the gun and built the complete bike in only four days. It took longer than that to do the sketches.

Day One:

It was about 6 a.m. when an old friend and auto designer, Jeff Teague, and I were at the shop ready to begin the design phase of the Secret Weapon project. He and I were in the process of slamming down a few cups of caffeine as I heard the gate alarm in the shop go off alerting us to the arrival of a visitor coming down the driveway. Judging by the continuous chirping of the siren, I could tell that it was either an idiot dancing in front of the motion sensor, or a very long vehicle was rolling in. Hopefully, it was the latter, since I was expecting delivery of the Boss Hoss motorcycle.

Knowing my new Boss Hoss was due at about this time, I went out to the shop to open the big roll-up door. On the other side was Victor Vert from California Boss Hoss in his crew cab truck. And hitched behind the truck was his Boss

Hoss transporter containing one new 350-cubic-inch V-8 motorcycle! The day was off to a fine start.

We unloaded the bike and I drove the beast into the shop as the crew gathered around to get a close look. I have a drawing table in the center of the shop and we gathered around it as I laid out the game strategy. The basic plan was to build a military bike that would stand out; something wild, but not too wild. Something that would get attention, but not the wrong kind of attention. Something that looked as if it were real, but also like something that had never been built before. But above all, it had to make the public smile when they saw it.

This was a tall order, but the biggest challenge was the fact that we had to build it in only five days (thanks to my big mouth). The clock started ticking from the moment the bike rolled into the shop. We were already into day one

This is the most critical point in a project and that is the teardown—the point where bolts and parts are lost. Here we have an empty workbench just waiting for parts.

and I knew we would not even start the actual build until day two at the earliest. I found that if you just jump into a project without a plan or without everyone on the same page, you have chaos, and chaos will do nothing but delay the project.

I started by getting everyone that was going to be involved in the build together and explained the requirements and design ideas I wanted to incorporate into this project. Jeff listened intently as he sketched out a few designs, and I also brought out a few props that I wanted to incorporate into the Secret Weapon. Rather than simply paint a custom bike with a red, white and blue color scheme like so many builders do, I decided that this bike should actually resemble some sort of military vehicle.

The night before, I had made a run to the bookstore to grab a few books about Marine vehicles. I had pictures of guns and bombs and the latest desert camouflage pattern and I brought all of the samples out during the meeting so that we could figure out how to incorporate it into the finished machine. By the end of day one we were organized, informed and each member of the crew had specific instructions or, in this case, "marching orders".

Day Two:

We concluded the first day at a fairly normal hour, but even with a full night's rest, day two came soon enough. It was 5 a.m. and I managed to beat the sun up again, but at that early hour, the shop was like a refrigerator and the grips of my tools felt like ice. However, the coffee was hot and we had a job to do with four days remaining to do it. I put a jacket on and started by taking off a few parts as I waited for the rest of the crew to arrive.

Jon Forseth is my machine shop foreman and head machinist. He started building the two mini-guns that would mount onto the front crash bars. Jon came to me about seven years ago for a job with a resumé heavy in roofing. He had also been a baggage checker at LAX. Not what you would consider material for a machinist, but he had a good attitude and a sense of humor, so I hired him and it didn't take long for him to become proficient at CNC fabrication.

Kelly was a girl that I met on the set of "Monster House." She was a member of the production team and kept me in plasma cutter tips and MIG wire as we built the Shark House for the show. Always keeping a watchful eye out for

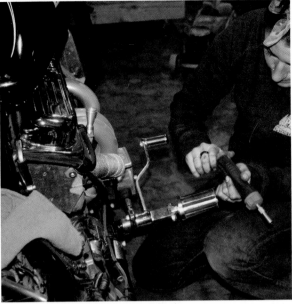

To hold the bike solid as we worked on it, we fabricated a set of blocks that attached to the top of the jack stands and bolted to the frame. This made the bike safer to work on.

Using good-quality tools will speed things up a bit.

The instrument panel was removed and the wires unplugged and labeled for reassembly. This allowed us to pull the gas tank.

talented people and potential employees, I handed her my card and told her to give me call if she wanted to work. She called me back about a year after the show aired and said she was interested in coming down for an interview. She was hired on in time to do some of the welding on Secret Weapon.

Bruce Busick is our shop mechanic and one of the two part-timers on the crew. He's married to Peggy, our receptionist, and has been with us through a few films now. Bruce comes in during the afternoon after putting in a full day at FedEx. He is a mechanical guru and general fabricator.

Jeff Tapley came to us through Moe D'Onofrio, our Snap-on Tool dealer. Jeff is a gaffer with a solid film background, but he also knows about bikes and welding. Plus, he's got plenty of good tools! So whenever Jeff is not on location doing his lighting thing, he comes in to work for me.

Mario Harders is another member of the crew who, like Jon, didn't come with special skills, but manages to adapt to whatever needs to be done. Mario caught on to CNC machining well enough to crank out the pseudo-bullets

We disconnected the fuel line at the tank and drained the tank for weight reduction as it holds up to 7 gallons at about 8 lbs. per gallon.

Removing the tank required disconnecting the fuel line and a bunch of wires from the dash. These wires had to be marked for reassembly at a later date.

The Secret Weapon—Our Mad Five-Day Thrash To Build The First "Ultimate Chopper"

Even the front fender had to be redone. The stock version did not match the Secret Weapon theme I had in mind for this bike.

that are part of the Secret Weapon armament.

Brian Hatano is my general manager who can handle just about anything out in the shop. He and I go way back to when I had my first customizing shop back in the '70s. He started by sweeping floors and rapidly worked his way to chief fabricator, head painter, body man and welder. One day, a brief boredom set in and he moved to what was then Peterson Publishing Company to work his way up to editor of *Drag Racing* magazine and senior editor of *Car Craft* magazine. As luck would have it, he returned and is back to painting, grinding, welding and writing for me. Apparently we offer more diversity and less boredom than he originally thought. Having been together for so long, Brian and I work well as a team on projects such as this. For this build, I designed and patterned while Brian took the patterns and fabricated, welded and painted.

When the crew was assembled, we finished taking everything off the bike such as the tank, fenders, windshield and seat. I decided that this was going to be a cosmetic conversion without any structural frame changes or engine modifications. However, the cosmetic changes that I had

We wrapped a chain around the frame and lifted the bike with a forklift as we slipped the jack stands under the frame.

We removed the rear foot pegs and used that mounting hole for the attachment point. You can see the modification to the jack stands.

By using jack stands we could adjust the height of the bike at any time we wanted.

planned would not be easy. The Boss Hoss has a large fuel tank and several panels that did not fit in with the military theme. Furthermore, all of the parts that we needed to make would have to fit the bike without drilling or modifying the existing frame in any way. This was just in case we wanted to return the bike back to its stock configuration after the show. (As it later turned out, the bike was a big hit and will more than likely remain the Secret Weapon.)

The most important step in a project for me is to decide upon and coordinate the modifications. Because of our short time frame, I did this while the bike was being disassembled. Since the plan was to convert the bike cosmetically, one of the most important decisions that had to be made concerned the paint job. Originally, I wanted to paint the whole bike in camouflage, including the wheels, front end and engine, but it was hard to bring myself to sand down all that beautiful chrome work that comes from the Boss Hoss factory. We decided to put off the chrome-verses-paint dilemma until later.

The bulletproof windshield that I planned on would be more than a cosmetic piece. Not only would it shield the rider from wind, but since it was to be constructed of 1/2-inch Makrolon polycarbonate plastic, the shield would actually deflect a bullet should the bike be exposed to hostile fire from the front. The shape would be multi-faceted with 2-inch-wide metal strips and polished stainless steel bolts joining each of the plastic panels together. The windshield alone seemed like a week's worth of work, and it had to be assembled and disassembled four times for the complete process of fabrication and painting.

The overall design of the bike would be a cross between a stealth bomber, an army tank and an arsenal on two wheels. As I got Bruce off to a good start on the windshield, I began to convert the design that Jeff Teague and I came up with on day one into working patterns for Brian to fabricate

The old windshield was removed and the mounting brackets taken off to be used on our new windshield.

with. Meanwhile, Jon started machining hand grenades and a pair of mini-guns, and Mario started making bullets—hundreds of them for the ammo belts that feed the mini-guns. Each bullet is an exact replica of the real thing because, even though it was a show bike, it had to look convincing. After all, it would be seen by the experts, the Marines!

I like to make my patterns out of either foam core or thin sheets of clear plastic, but on this radiator shroud foam core was the better choice because it was stronger.

One big advantage with foam core is that you can cut it with a razor knife and don't need any fancy or costly equipment.

Day Three:

The body shape (I refer to it as a body because the panels of the Boss Hoss cover a large portion of the framework) was a design in progress. It kind of developed itself as we progressed. As I patterned one panel, the contiguous panel sort of designed itself. I began with the windshield and the faceted design flowed rearward into the other parts of the bike. All I had to do was hold the template material up to the bike and I could literally see where to bend it and where to cut it. Of course, this is an oversimplification, but the point is that the hardest part is just getting started.

I made the templates, or patterns, out of cardboard. Then, after bending the temporary piece to fit, the design was transferred to a sheet of 18- or 20-gauge sheet metal. The template like this must be trimmed and creased until a precision fit is attained before transferring the pattern to metal. Each pattern goes through several trial fittings, and once I'm sure that it looks and fits properly, I trace the shape onto the sheet metal, cut it and bend it to match the template. It is much easier to cut and shape cardboard than

Jeff works on a mounting bracket as I finish a pattern for the radiator shell.

metal, so if you do as much trimming and fitting with the template, you'll save time and money in the metal working stage. Some "fabricators" feel that working with templates is a waste of time. It's not, but we'll get into the details of pattern work later.

The design of the Secret Weapon's two mini-guns is something that some people might recognize from the movie *xXx*. The heavily armed GTO driven in the film by actor Vin Diesel was designed and built here in my shop. Since the GTO was a stunt car, I not only had to build back-up cars, but also back-up armament for each car including rockets, grenades and mini-guns. So the guns on the Secret Weapon are actually extra props from *xXx* that were taking up space in my office.

Although the two guns were pieces that were already made, they were not direct bolt-ons for the Secret Weapon. Jon suggested that we mount the guns to the side of the crash bars, rather than to the tank area as I planned. We all went around and around about it and I had to admit that

Most patterns can be flipped over to make the opposite side of the part, so I often mark "right side" on one side and "left side" on the other side.

The Secret Weapon—Our Mad Five-Day Thrash To Build The First "Ultimate Chopper"

Another nice thing about working with foam core is that you can score (cut part way through) one side and bend the panel on the cut, which is how you will bend the metal indicating the final shape and giving you the location of the bend on the pattern.

I have most of the patterns made and in place to check for fit as Jeff checks his front tank mount bracket. Pattern making can go quickly, but I have been doing this for many years.

Once the pattern is finished, you can proceed to making the metal part. The way I look at it, if the pattern fits, the part has to fit, too.

Brian uses a jigsaw with a metal cutting blade to cut out the metal. I like electric sheet metal shears, so your choice of tools should depend on what you feel comfortable with. There is no perfect tool for everything.

they did look better there, so I added the idea of linking the guns together so they would swivel from side to side in unison. When it comes to ideas, every member of my crew constantly tries to outdo each other. Depending on the work at hand, this can be a good thing or a bad thing. In this case, a good idea came out of it. More importantly, when I come up with an idea and the rest of my crew tries to "one-up" me with a better idea, it keeps us all sharp.

The mounting of the bullets was the next thing to be considered. I had a few belts of blanks that were left over from a war movie we once did. I started to use them, but quickly changed my mind when I realized that the bike would be on the show car circuit and there was a chance that someone might hit a primer and set one off. So it was back to the machine department to get Mario and Jon started on making the 200 bullets from brass bar stock. The bullets would be retrofitted into the ammo belts that I had, along with red-tipped tracer rounds in place just like the real thing. The ammo belts and a brace of grenades would be ready by the end of day four.

Here's a trade secret: The parts almost never fit perfectly the first time. We have to fit them as many as three times to get a perfect fit, trimming and tweaking along the way. made notes on the finished side panel. such as the 5-mark indicating that I should bend the crease up 5 degrees.

Day Four:

It was getting down to crunch time (whatever that is!), and even though everyone was hard at work, there were still some major design issues to solve. Actually, it was the fuel tank that was the stumbling block. The choices were: use the factory Boss Hoss tank, which was the easiest, but the least appealing as far as creating a military-style was concerned. The second alternative was to build a new tank incorporating the angular "stealth" silhouette that I envisioned. This would be my choice if it weren't for the self-imposed five-day time constraint that we were faced with. So, after kicking around a few ideas, Brian came up with option number three, and the one that we went with.

During the initial design session, we decided to equip the Secret Weapon with an auxiliary supply of fuel in the form of Army-style Gerry cans that would mount onto the Boss Hoss frame where a pair of saddlebags would normally be placed. Most military vehicles have a high-rate of fuel consumption and the V-8-powered Boss Hoss

Jeff makes a slight adjustment in a bracket for the rear fender mount. Jeff is our "meticulous one," measure 10 times and cut once.

The Secret Weapon—Our Mad Five-Day Thrash To Build The First "Ultimate Chopper"

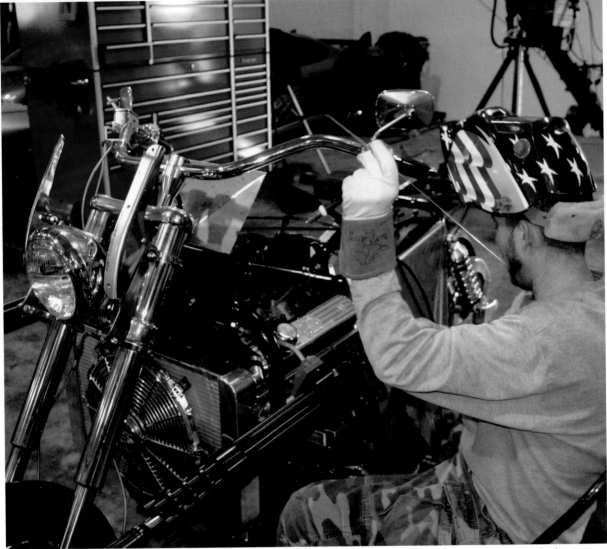

Jeff welds the tank mounts in place and things are going well. Jeff prefers TIG over MIG welding and it does reduce (eliminate) splatter.

The radiator shroud is finished. I added louvers to hide the radiator and make it look more bulletproof. The foam core can simply be taped in place with masking tape and cut apart when you need to remove it.

would be no different. After a quick evaluation of the fuel pump capability and feasibility of routing the lines from the rear of the bike to the Holley Fuel Injection system, Brian determined that using the Gerry cans as the primary source of fuel was doable, so we proceeded to do it.

So the factory fuel tank was permanently set aside and I designed a stealth-style structure that would fill the void left by the removal of the big stock tank. Rather than holding fuel, this new sleek structure would contain electronics for the weaponry, communications, and tracking that are commonplace on such an assault vehicle. As fast as I could pattern the structure and the remaining panels of the bodywork, Brian cut, shaped and welded the pieces into place.

In the meantime, Jeff and Kelly moved to the rear of the bike to begin fabricating a frame that would be strong enough to hold the two Gerry cans with fuel securely to the side of the bike. Trial-fitting the cans in place showed us that each can would have to be notched to clear the swing arm movement. Modifying the Gerry cans turned into the proverbial open can of worms. Cutting a relief into the side

We had a set of Gatling (Vulcan) guns lying around and this was the perfect project for the little "poppers." Jon made a set of mounts and we were off and running… uh, shooting.

Brian slips in a panel on the front fender. We made the fender out of separate sections to add strength and a certain look I wanted.

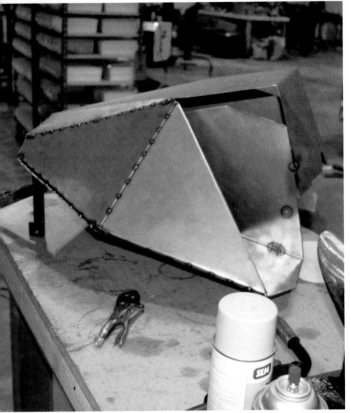

The tank is coming together one piece at a time. We first built a section for the right side and then a section for the left side off the same pattern, helping keep the symmetry of the design.

We did what we call an "intermittent" tack weld. With this we lay down a spot and skip about a half inch and then lay down another spot and continue along the entire seam. This keeps the heat from welding down to a minimum. We normally fill in the gaps later, but in this instance we liked the look and decided to keep it this way.

At this stage I almost decided to leave the front of the tank open as it looked like a set of intake scoops on a jet.

We transferred the pattern to metal and used the Milwaukee sheers cut it out. This piece will be the center section of the rear fender.

Even with the new technique of welding we still have to "encourage the metal" to move in line with its contiguous panels.

of each can and shaping a patch panel was not a problem, but the simple process of welding to the cans proved to be a headache. We found out that the cans are assembled with lead solder, a material that conflicts with normal welding.

So Kelly did her best to weld as close to the leaded areas as she could and I devised a way to seal the seams that might pose a problem with leakage. The idea was good, but as the saying goes: The operation was a success, but the patient died. The idea was to cover the seams with a little JB Weld, then hook up a vacuum pump to the fuel line fitting that we installed and pull a little vacuum. In theory, the vacuum would pull the JB Weld into the seam and seal the opening. The idea worked, but a little too much vacuum was applied and the sides of the first Gerry can collapsed. Brian and I stepped in and quickly reshaped the damaged can while Jeff and Kelly repeated the procedure on the remaining can, but with more discretion on the vacuum sealing process. By the end of the day, all fabrication was complete, all accessories were mounted, and the Secret Weapon was ready for paint.

I wouldn't put gas in it, but it is ready for the paint shop and Brian's touch, which will finish it off.

At this point we added the two 5-gallon tanks to the rear of the bike for the real fuel supply.

A finished belt of ammo.

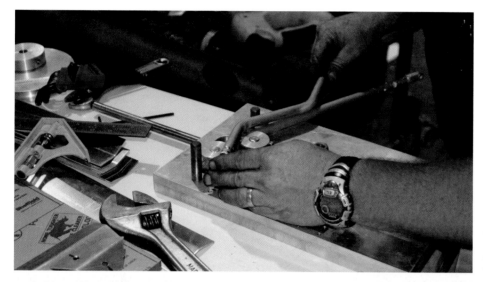

We don't seem to do anything the easy way. If we need a tube bent, we design and build a tube bender. In this case, we needed a set of rods to connect the guns together so they would both turn the same direction and be linked together.

The Secret Weapon—Our Mad Five-Day Thrash To Build The First "Ultimate Chopper"

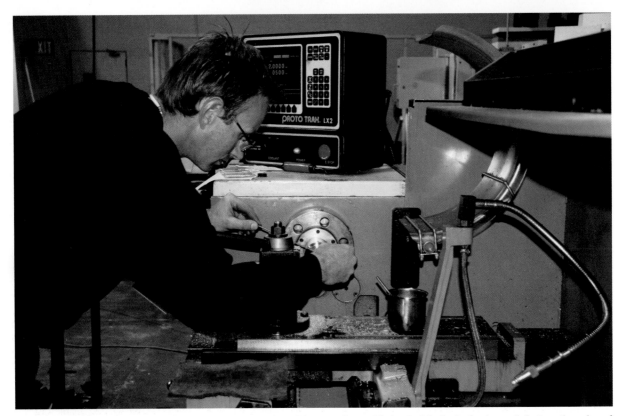

As Jon was making grenades, Mario was turning out bullets (literally) on another CNC lathe. Each bullet had to be made by inserting a bar of brass into the lathe and turning one end, then removing it and turning the other end. Each bullet took about five minutes. With about 400 bullets, this process equaled about 33 hours of work. Mario was busy.

Each grenade was tested by the "pull the pin and wait 7 seconds" test. When asked if they are real, I say, "only one is."

When making a steel bracket, we sometimes use a welding rod for a pattern, bending it to fit in the area we need. We then use this as a "bend pattern" to show us the angle of the bend and the length of each section.

Once the welding rod dimensions are transferred to a piece of steel bar, the bar can be bent and held up against the bike to double check the fit.

This may not be the best way to hold a bracket while grinding, but we often break a few rules when we are racing against the clock. Here, Jeff is only removing a few-thousands of an inch from a bracket.

A CNC mill comes in handy for a job like this, but is not required. I have built hundreds of bikes and cars without one, although, if you have one it will sure save a lot of time.

I used to do all my bending with a torch and a vice, but now that I have a hydraulic bender we get consistent fast bends that are very repeatable.

The rear tank bracket is in place and ready for the front bracket to be fabricated.

You can just see the front bracket in front of Jeff's face. Try to use the existing bolts of any car or bike when mounting anything onto the vehicle.

The Secret Weapon—Our Mad Five-Day Thrash To Build The First "Ultimate Chopper"

The top section of the tank is fabricated and tack welded to the tank mounting brackets just to give added strength and support to the structure. This piece can now be removed as a unit and the rest of the tank built on a bench.

The start of the project involved the acquisition of two 5-gallon gas cans and the trays they sit in.

The bottom of the tank would hit the swing arm if the tanks were mounted close to the bike, but if mounted far enough away to clear they would look bad and make the back of the bike too wide. The only option was to cut and modify each of the tanks and mounting trays.

We added a piece of metal to the bottom to fill in the gap that we cut out.

The tanks were added and checked for clearance and mounting options.

We made a fitting to cover the gas filler spout and added a bit of air pressure (no more than about 2 psi). The outside of the weld was covered with soapy water to help us look for leaks.

The gas cans clear the suspension and swing arm. Now they can be tested for leaks.

Aluminum diamond plate was then cut to act as tank shields and a means of attaching the mounting bar.

I designed a simple way of mounting the tanks on the bike so they would not fall off. This involved little more than a steel rod through the handles of the cans.

The plates fit as if they were made for the job.

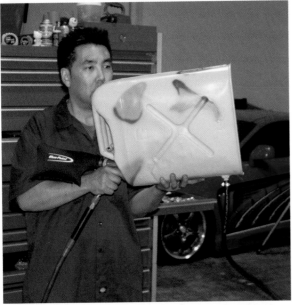

After paint, the tanks had to be vacuumed out so we would not gum up the engine with contaminates from the painting and welding.

The fuel tank project is almost complete.

Mounted, painted and ready to see some action, the tanks looked as good as they worked. They also give the bike a longer range due to the increased fuel capacity.

Our windshield is held in place with a few clamps as I work on it. This allows me to remove it for quick modifications.

When making two patterns that are the same, you can sometimes flip the foam core over and use it for the opposite side.

As each piece is added, the whole windshield gets much stronger because it is becoming a compound form. This is the same reason cardboard is corrugated—it adds more strength without adding a lot more weight.

With the patterns in place, the design of the bike starts to take shape.

The pattern is almost finished and strong enough to support the load as I start making brackets that will fit at the seams of the Makrolon (the material that the windshield will be made from).

I have even marked the areas in which I will later add brackets that will hold the plastic together.

Brian used SEM self-etching primer on the parts we have fabricated. He says it is much faster than loading a gun for a small part.

The inside is covered with an undercoating and left to dry.

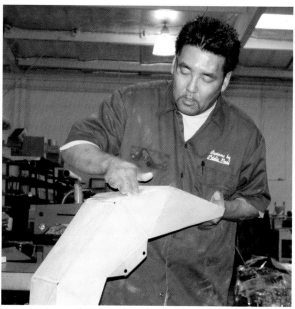

Once dry, the outside of the front fender is sanded to a smooth finish and set aside for the base coat of paint.

Now we sand the side panels inside and out for the base coat, making sure that they are primed first with a good primer and every inch of the metal is covered.

Day Five:

Painting camouflage may look simple but to do it per military specifications is a little more involved than just shooting patches of green and brown color. Since our objective was to create a realistic military bike, I decided to look into the art of camouflage. I soon discovered that there are specific colors and patterns for each branch of the military, and the specifics break down even more, depending on where the camouflaged vehicle will be put into action. A Web search provided me with the pre-digital Gulf War-style that looked simple enough to adapt to the

Secret Weapon panels.

With all pattern work complete, I began fabrication of the last remaining panel—a louvered shroud to cover and protect the radiator. Brian shifted into paint mode and began prepping each piece for the base color. The Gulf War camouflage consisted of four basic colors: a sand-toned base with a combination of rock- and dirt-colored patterns.

Our teamwork really showed during the last two days of the build. As I completed the shroud, Brian had the remaining panels, tank structure and Gerry cans coated with the base color. While the shroud was being painted, I dusted off my Badger Airbrushes and began applying

The Secret Weapon—Our Mad Five-Day Thrash To Build The First "Ultimate Chopper"

No one really sells Camouflage paint, so we had to pick and mix the colors to match a panel we had.

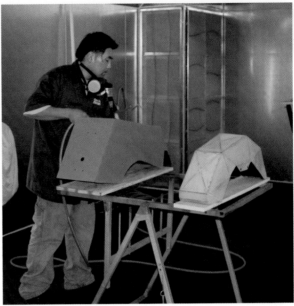

We spray air on the parts to get rid of any dust that may be hiding in the corners waiting to come out and mess up a good paint job.

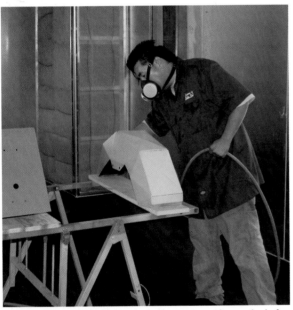

The base coat is applied using the half-pattern overlap method of spraying, where each spray pattern is lapped over the previous pattern by 50 percent.

The tank fits like a glove as it is lowered onto the mounting brackets.

the intricate scheme of colors to simulate the desert camouflage. While expanding my business over the years, I still manage to keep myself out in the shop with my hands in the projects. While I'm usually involved more on the fabricating end these days, painting is something that I used to do on a regular basis and still enjoy doing whenever I have the chance.

My favorite part of any project is completing it and watching everything come together. At certain stages of building a car or a bike, it seems as if the job is taking forever no matter how fast we move. And with a pending deadline of just five days, that can add up to a lot of stress!

The Secret Weapon build was not without the typical problems encountered during custom fabrication, but fortunately, there were no major snags or setbacks.

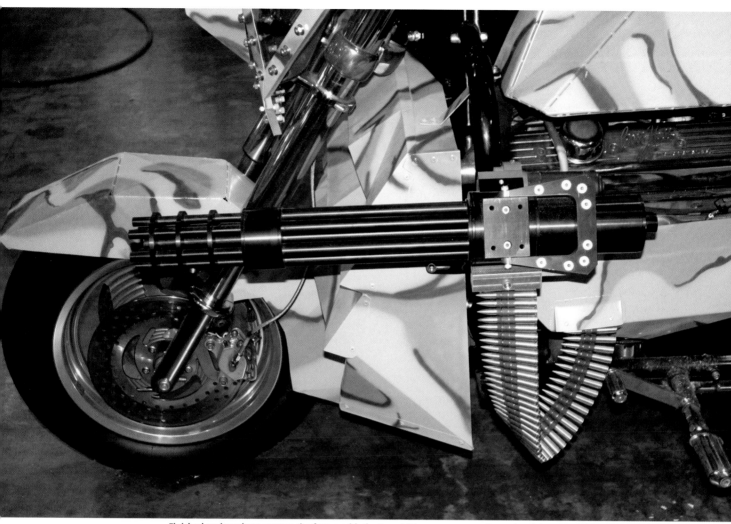

Finished and ready to protect the free world, the Secret Weapon was now "armed and dangerous."

The bike is almost ready for the show circuit. We made the ammo belts hang so you can turn the guns.

A lot of what we did on this bike will never be seen because it is under the panels and seat, but without the attention to detail the bike would not be "built right." A theme bike like this has to run as good as it looks.

The Secret Weapon—Our Mad Five-Day Thrash To Build The First "Ultimate Chopper"

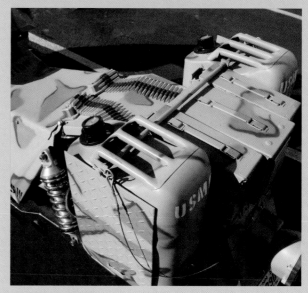

A not-so-secret weapon!

With the Secret Weapon complete and loaded onto a trailer, it was off to the show, where we would find out soon enough if our military theme and five days of hard work were a success. The first scheduled appearance was the Motor Trend Auto Show in San Diego, California. The Secret Weapon was a featured attraction that stole the show away from all the new cars and our other featured vehicle, the '93 Toyota Supra from the movie *2Fast 2Furious*.

Show promoter Skip Johnson showed up at the booth and informed me that the Secret Weapon was so popular that it had to be at the next three shows in San Jose, California, Salt Lake City, Utah, and Omaha, Nebraska. And as soon as it was back from the Motor Trend show circuit, the bike would be part of the Boss Hoss exhibit at the Laughlin, Nevada, bike run, where the hardest of the hardcore bikers would see it for the first time.

The Secret Weapon—Our Mad Five-Day Thrash To Build The First "Ultimate Chopper"

Chapter Two

Frame Fabrication—The Foundation of Chopper One

This is Jay Leno's brand-new 502 Boss Hoss that we had in the shop for a custom paint job. We also used it to measure and photograph for reference as we proceeded onwards into uncharted territory. Thanks, Jay!

Frame Geometry Made Simple

The frame of a motorcycle determines the three most important factors in the overall design: strength/rigidity, style and handling characteristics. Actually, the frame is the foundation of all vehicles, but when the plan is to harness more than 1,000 horsepower on two wheels, the fabrication of the frame is not something that you want to compromise for either style or cost. Therefore, the frame of Chopper One had to be constructed of the strongest materials and designed specifically for the engine that would be used for the bike; in this case, a big-block Chevy V-8 with two superchargers. The factory Boss Hoss frame for the 502-inch Chevy engine is a well-engineered piece that, like the small-block 350-inch V-8 version, would be a good starting point for this build. However, I wanted to incorporate two features on Chopper One for which the factory frame would have to be extensively modified in order to accommodate. For this reason, I decided to build my own frame.

The photos in this chapter will tell the story of how we fabricated the Chopper One frame better than the text, but what you might not be able to see is what we went through to get the job done within our time schedule.

Due to the fact that my shop has numerous jobs in progress at all times, the process of fabricating this frame was interrupted frequently. I can't provide an accurate time for building the Chopper One frame, but an educated guess would put us in the area of about four days with Brian, my shop manager and main fabricator, and I working on it. Now, four days might seem long to some people, but keep in mind that we also had to stop at regular intervals for the photographs that you see here along with working on other jobs in the shop. But a build like this certainly doesn't have to be done that fast for the average guy. One of the reasons we can build so fast is that we have full in-house capability to do everything in one shop. We do not have to send out any parts for machining, bending, or welding and wait for its return, like you might need to do.

When you build a custom motorcycle frame, keep in mind that every component on the bike relates to the frame. For instance, the kickstand must be located within the rider's reach and the extension of the stand determines how the bike leans; if it leans too far, it could snap the kickstand and fall over. If it does not lean enough, a slight bump can tip the bike on its side. Can you turn the front end from lock to lock without hitting the gas tank, or can you change the oil and oil filter without having to pull the engine? The message here is to plan ahead when fabricating

A good tool for frame fabrication is a set of angle/radius gauges that will allow you to set up a tube and accurately angle it to the tube you are bending. Each radius gauge is designed for a different bend radius.

a custom frame so there will be no surprises after the bike is completed and assembled.

When it comes to choppers, a custom frame usually involves modifying the rake, or angle of the neck (measured in degrees); and/or extending the overall length by stretching the top cross tube. The **neck tube** is the starting point for custom frame fabrication. By the way, frame terminology tends to vary from one builder to the next, so a brief description of each frame component might be helpful.

The neck tube is the part of the frame in which the fork assembly is installed. The cross tube or tubes are sometimes referred to as the backbone. The **cross tube** is the top portion of the frame that connects the neck to the rear section. A motorcycle frame may have one or two **down tubes** depending on the particular design, and these connect from the lower part of the neck and travel down under the engine to the rear section.

At first glance, all motorcycles might appear to be identical in terms of frame design; however, there are several different frame styles that exist depending on the type of bike. As far as custom choppers are concerned, though, the basic frame

If you are going to perform more than one bend in a single tube, you will need one of these little clamp-on levels to keep the tube level and to apply the proper amount of rotation before making subsequent bends.

Chopper Building and Liability

One thing that often gets overlooked by chopper builders is, who is liable for a bike that doesn't handle or perform as good as it should or, worse yet, for damage or injuries that result from the modifications that have been made to the bike? While the answer might be obvious, let me say that I know that the second I cut into the existing bike, I take on all the liability for any modification that I make, whether it's simply poor handling characteristics, breakage or injury. Unless you too are willing to take on the responsibility of liability, don't even think about making your own custom frame. Just read this chapter for your own edification and how it is done by others.

Unfortunately, we seem to be living in an age in which no one accepts responsibility for what they do. Unless this changes, the hobby of customizing and custom bikes will soon be complicated with more insurance issues and lawsuits.

is either suspended or rigid with one or two down tubes. Other styles such as the monocoque, perimeter, or trellis frame are used mainly for racing and foreign (European and Japanese) bikes. Of course, the Boss Hoss with its V-8 power plant doesn't really fall into any existing category as far as factory frame design goes. Still, the stock Boss Hoss frame is similar to the Harley-Davidson with two exceptions: size (the Hoss frame is much larger) and, due to the big engine, it has two-piece construction to allow for installation of the engine and transmission. We'll get into this a little later.

All Boss Hoss bikes have suspended frames from the factory. "Suspended" means that the rear section incorporates a swingarm and shock absorber assembly. For a cushy ride on a touring bike, having rear suspension is nice. But a chopper really isn't a chopper unless it has a rigid frame. That's why it was an absolute necessity for me to un-suspend my Boss Hoss frame for the build-up of Chopper One.

Another frame modification that I needed to make was to increase the clearance at the front of the engine for the supercharger drive. But in order to maintain the original profile of the Boss Hoss, which I feel looks good to begin with, I had to perform this modification without deviating too much from the stock 82-inch wheelbase. Realizing that things could get complicated very quickly, I got out the measuring tape and drew up a rough blueprint of the frame dimensions that I needed. One of my objectives was to keep the design as simple as possible.

To simplify the design of my custom frame, I chose to stick to the Boss Hoss design wherever possible. I would use the same type and size of tubing (1.5-inch O.D. x .120-inch wall thickness, seamless chrome-moly); I would keep the rake at a mild 33 degrees, which is standard for both small- and big-block Boss Hoss frames; and I would splice my frame near the same locations on the tubes that Boss Hoss does, but substitute the frame tube connectors with my own design. After taking some rough measurements on the stock Boss Hoss frame, I found that I needed

approximately 5 inches of additional clearance at the front of the engine to accommodate the supercharger drive assembly. So, to avoid affecting the length of the wheelbase, I would simply shorten the rear section by 5 inches to offset the stretch at the front. Since I was also going rigid with the frame, there wouldn't be any complications with re-engineering the length of the swingarm; it would be totally removed.

Prior to bending any tubing, I talked the guys at Boss Hoss into sending me one of their cast steel neck pieces. This heavy-duty part is used on all of the factory frames and would serve as a reference point for the measurements that I needed to make. The Boss Hoss neck piece incorporates saddles for the top tubes and down tubes to attach to. This established the stock 33-degree fork rake without having to make any measurements, and once the tubes were seated into each saddle, this gave us an accurate starting point with correct alignment. Since I planned to go with the factory fork assembly on Chopper One, using this piece as a starting point for my custom frame was a big time saver.

The Chopper One frame consists of 10 tubes welded together. Six of those tubes required no less than five bends to contour around the big engine and meet at the rear section. The rear section would be a rigid design with the top and bottom frame tubes ending in a set of four parallel extensions, each one tipped with a '59 Cadillac-style tail light. Each of the tubes will have to be custom bent and twisted into a one-off configuration around a big engine with dual superchargers, a special transmission, and a fat 300mm rear tire. And all of this has to be accomplished while maintaining a style and flow that must remain consistent with the overall design and theme of the bike.

At this point, we were ready to start the design and fabrication of the new rigid frame. The initial design of the frame was developed on computer using AutoCAD software. AutoCAD drawings can be printed for use as a reference during fabrication, and the data can also be converted to a CAM file for CNC mill and lathe work when the time comes. Of course, using AutoCAD is not

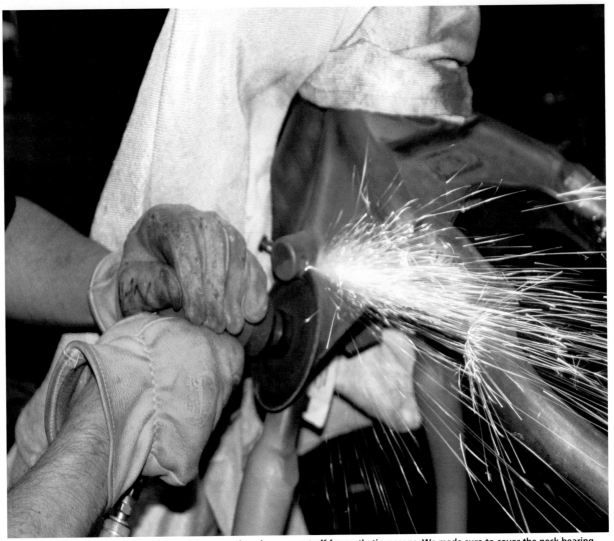

Portions of the stock neck, such as the crash bar mounting plugs, are cut off for aesthetic reasons. We made sure to cover the neck bearing races to avoid getting weld spatter on them or grinding dust in them.

a requirement for building a motorcycle frame, but it's the way we do all of our work here at Customs By Eddie Paul. The do-it-yourself equivalent of the CAD process is to simply take a tape measure and start measuring each part of the frame and write down exactly what tubing lengths you'll need to cut. As I mentioned earlier, everything relates to the frame, so you'll need to have a clear idea of what goes where when designing each part of the frame. If you plan to build your own frame, my recommendation is to make a checklist of all parts and critical areas of the frame that must be considered in the design.

When building a custom frame based on an existing design, the first thing to do is start by taking dimensions from the original frame. These basic dimensions include:

➤ Distance from the neck to the engine

➤ Distance from the neck to the rear of the transmission

➤ Distance from the neck to the rear axle

When taking these measurements, it's important to have a common point to start each measurement from. This common point or points must be used for measuring out the new frame tubes. I used a hole in the frame that the

fork stop bolt screws into for the datum point, and from this hole I took as many measurements as I could. Since the neck piece for the new frame is exactly the same as the one on the existing frame, all of my measurements could be transferred to and from it with accuracy during the fabrication.

Another thing to take into account is the load on the suspension. If measurements are taken on a frame with the bike resting on its kickstand, the partial load taken off the suspension will more than likely render a false reading. The difference might not be critical, but standing the bike upright and off the kickstand will minimize some variables. I also took all the body parts off the bike so I could measure the frame as accurately as possible; this not only facilitates the measuring process, but it also reveals details such as mounting brackets and flanges that I would need to re-fabricate onto the new frame.

Starting with the down tubes, I began to calculate the length of each tube for the new frame. With pen and paper at my side, I took notes of the length of each tube as well as the location and degree of the bends. I like to make a rough hand sketch with callouts for length pointing to

After we bend each tube, it is then taken to the donor bike and checked for "gross" measurements and angles. This will indicate whether we are close or way off track early in the venture. This is also checked with the neck casting for angle and fit before duplication of the other side of the frame.

each tube. As critical as this step is, it didn't take long for me to measure out each tube for the new frame. Then I took my rough sketch and measurements into my office and pulled up the AutoCAD program on my PC. With AutoCAD, I can convert my rough set of plans into a neat and easy-to-read blueprint visual of what I was about to do. On the computer, you can shrink, stretch, move and lower a bike with ease, and once you have the finished look, the dimensions on the drawing can be entered into the Bend Calculator program to determine where and how much to make your bends. For those who are computer savvy enough, you can easily develop your own bending calculator on a spreadsheet program such as Microsoft Excel. Once I ran my dimensions on the Bend Calculator, I printed out the results that provided the numeric bend points and angles of the bends, and then I headed out into the shop.

Once the design of the frame is established, individual frame tubes can be pulled up from the drawing with specs indicating measurements and bend degrees. With this information, I was able to place an order with my metal supplier, M&K Metals in Gardena, California, for the amount of seamless (also referred to as DOM, or drawn-over-mandrel) tubing that I would need. Although the metal supplier can cut metal to an exact length, I prefer to order in bulk because I never know exactly what length I'm going to need for a particular job. Each of the tubes that I ordered for Chopper One came in 10-foot lengths. I planned to make as many bends as possible on a flat plain to keep the job simple. I knew, though, that some of the bends would require some three-dimensional thinking at some point.

The size of the tubing was to be 1.50 inches in diameter with an 0.120-inch wall thickness. The frame is the main support for the big engine as well as everything else, so it had to be strong. According to my AutoCAD drawing, I would have to make several precise bends on each tube. Whenever a bike is custom-built from scratch such as the

With the lower frame tubes off the bike, the rear wheel is mocked up just for giggles and to get a rough idea of where it is and what will be required to make it fit where we want it. The whole process of an extreme chopper build is repeated teardowns and reassemblies. Everything has to fit before the frame is ready for paint.

Chopper One is, it's advisable to have some kind of sketch or computer drawing printed out to refer to during the construction process. Not only did I have my AutoCAD printout, but I also had a beautiful color rendition (see page 94) of what the finished bike might look like created by my artist friend Jeff Teague of Teague Design. Jeff is one of those artists who can literally take a verbal description of a bike or car and convert it into a very detailed concept illustration. Not only does this provide a visual for the build, but also a nice conversation piece to frame and hang on the wall when the project is finished.

Applying a bend to steel tubing with a .120-inch or greater wall thickness requires hydraulic machinery. While manual (hand pump) hydraulic benders are much more affordable and will bend heavy tubing up to .090 inch, there is no substitute for a hydraulic mandrel bender such as the Mittler Bros. 180-degree model in my shop. The MB bender uses a pedal-controlled 25-ton Enerpac Ram, CNC-machined aluminum shoes (mandrels) for bending different tube diameters, and a digital readout for accurate repeatability of bends. A handy accessory to the 180-degree

bending machine is the MB Bend Calculator software. The Bend Calculator is a Windows-based program that provides very accurate bend starting points when fed the correct information.

Another useful hydraulic bending machine in the shop is the Bentec BT-1000 made by Kiffer Industries, Inc. This is the tool that we use to bend bar stock into brackets and things. It can also bend tubing, but I prefer to dedicate each machine for specific tasks to minimize downtime from changing setups and tooling.

But even with all the latest state-of-the-art equipment in my shop, we still ran into a stumbling block right out of the gate. Although the MB Bend Calculator could calculate bends with a 4-inch radius for 1.50-inch tubing, the mandrels that we had for the bender would only accommodate an 8-inch radius. As time was not on our side, I didn't have the luxury of placing an order and waiting for new shoes to arrive from MB. I did, however, have the luxury of my CNC machine shop and a supply of aluminum plate and bar stock, so I did what any red-blooded American that owns his own machine shop

It was at this point that I noticed the frame was wider than intended by almost half an inch. Since there are many ways to widen a narrow frame, but few ways to narrow a wide frame, I thought I would rely on some technology from the ancient world. It was the Romans who discovered that by simply twisting a rope you could shorten the length between the two ends with great leverage. In any event, the frame was now back in perfect alignment and the rope was back in my toolbox.

would do in this situation: I built my own set of 4-inch-radius mandrels for 1.50 tubing. Actually, I delegated this to my machinist, Jon Forseth, who used some 6061-T6 aluminum plate and bar to make the new shoe and follow bar for the bender.

With the aluminum cut to size and the Fadal CNC warmed up, we started making chips fly, and it did not take long for the finished shoe and follow bar to go to deburring and then onto the bender for the first series of bends and a test of our skill. Since the new mandrels were "homemade," I decided to make a few trial bends on the 180-degree machine with some scrap tubing before starting in on the frame. The new tooling worked as good as the factory MB shoes and were deemed worthy of joining the ranks with the rest of our mandrels. My machine was now capable of producing a 4-inch bend radius and I was ready to start on the frame.

My plan was for the frame for Chopper One to be a true custom piece; one of a kind and never to be made again for any reason. Since I would never be making one of these frames again, I decided against taking the time to fabricate a full-on permanent fixture or jig. A perfectionist, or someone without a business to run might not agree, but with over three decades worth of bike- and car-building experience to back me up, I simply didn't feel that it was worth the time. When the time came to weld up the frame, I would make a lightweight temporary fixture to hold the tubes in place. A permanent frame jig is normally for building multiple frames, and constructing such a fixture is actually more expensive and time consuming than building the frame itself.

My plan was to cut and bend all of the tubing and mock up the custom frame before taking the engine out of the stock Boss Hoss frame. This way, I would have a reference for my measurements and the parts needed to make brackets. Once the new frame was tack welded together, I would strip down the Boss Hoss and transfer the engine and parts into the new frame for a trial fit, adjusting and moving brackets until everything fit perfectly.

I cut the tubing to the length required by the bend program and marked the points for the bends, as well as the amount of bend in degrees. The frame's down-tubes were

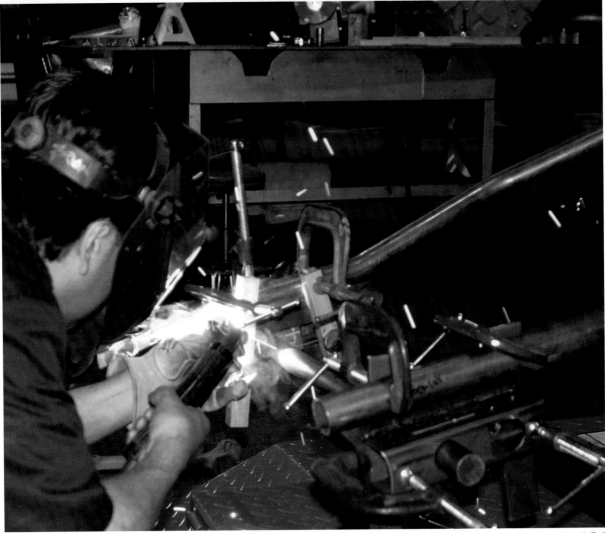

Now that the frame was in proper alignment the axle was added and the axle plates clamped for welding. This is known as a "poor man's jig" and is a way to align a sub component for welding by using the parts that have to fit together. It's simple and effective for a one-off project such as Chopper One.

put in the tubing bender one at a time and the first bend was made according to the dimensions given by the MB Bend Calculator. So far so good! I used a large MB protractor to check the degree of each bend, but one thing that neither the Bend Calculator nor the protractor can predict is the amount of spring-back after releasing the hydraulic pressure of the machine. Spring-back is the tension that the tubing retains when a bend is made. On the average, the amount of spring-back for the 1.5-inch tubing was about 2 degrees, which meant that to achieve a 90-degree bend, I would have to over-bend until the digital readout read 92 degrees. The amount of spring-back is not always the same. Spring-back is dependant on the diameter, wall, degree and type of steel you are bending. So what I often do is take a piece of the same tubing that I will be using on a project and do a practice bend of about 90 degrees and then mark the amount of spring-back on the tube for future reference. If you save the piece of tubing you will have a reference later if you bend the same type of tube.

The next bends were to be about 27 degrees, one bend upward and the other downward 27 degrees, so I marked it as a negative 27 degrees telling me that it is to be bent downward from the other bends. By bending the second bend 27 degrees up and the third bend down 27 degrees, I would wind up with the last piece parallel to the frame's bottom tube. This is exactly what I wanted. The bottom tube tilted out about ten degrees and if I wanted to complicate things, I could rotate the last two bends about 10 degrees on the main tube axis before I bent them. With the aid of a clamp-on digital level attached to the end of the frame tube, I rotated the tubing for the last bend until I saw 10 degrees on the level. Then I held the protractor next to the tube at the shoe and stepped on the pedal to start the bender in motion. After a few seconds, the frame tube was finished and measured out to exactly what I needed.

Now all I had to do was duplicate the tube for the other side. Duplicating the other side tube means that all dimensions and measurements will remain the same,

The bottom rear tubes are added and the rear axle plates are aligned and welded with the axle in place to guarantee perfect alignment.

however (and this is a big "however"!), it must be an opposite of the first tube. That means bends to the left are made to the right, and upward bends go down. If I've lost you, I doubt you are alone because this can get extremely confusing. I have often scrapped a tube because I bent up instead of down or in instead of out… or…well, you get the picture. So far, I have never found a foolproof way to mark the tube so that I would not have to concentrate on each of the bends. (If you know of one, write to me and let me know!) The best way for me to indicate which way to bend the tube is to mark the tube all the way around in black ink at the bend point, and then put a red dot or circle on the top side of the tube that should be bent. This way you have to rotate the tube to see the red mark which will also remind you that the tube has to be a certain rotation. I have also put the number of degrees that the tube should be bent at the same point so that I had to rotate the tube to see the amount of bend.

As each section of the frame is fabricated, the ends must also be notched with equal precision so that the edges of

One again the tire is located and measured to see if everything is going as smoothly as it looks. I opted for a 300mm rear tire for better traction, as well as looks.

Frame Fabrication—The Foundation of Chopper One

At first it looked like the engine might fit, but on a closer inspection we found the valve covers were hitting the top frame rails. This was not a catastrophe, though, because the frame could be notched and reinforced. Properly done, it would look as if the frame was wrapped tightly around the engine.

Once a frame rail is cut or modified in any way it should be made much stronger at that point or it could be a source of weakness. We added a solid piece of 1-inch steel bar inside the notched tube and a second 1 1/2-inch tube grafted to the inside of the frame rail.

Top-Notch Notching

The Scotchman GN6DE is a precision belt-type notcher that is easy to use and produces clean notches that are perfect for frame fabrication.

With the end of the tube notched to the right diameter and angle, the fit for welding is perfect.

I would have to say that one of the more time-consuming steps of fabrication with steel tubing is getting the ends properly notched. Time consuming, that is, if you don't have the proper equipment. A notch, in this case, is a radius or radii that must be cut at the end of the tube in order for it to butt up against another tube. The fit must be precise (no gaps) and the angle of the tube must be correct or the dimensions of the frame that you're building will be distorted. Notching is also required when fabricating a roll cage or a tubular chassis for a race car.

Methods of notching the end of a tube range from crude to acceptable to precision. Crude methods, such as

using a torch or an abrasive grinder, can actually yield a decent notch if you take the time to be neat about it. A vise-mounted hole-saw notcher is the most affordable tool made for notching, but it has a few drawbacks. Cheap import models are just that, cheap. A good vise-mount notcher will cost a couple hundred dollars. You'll still need a fairly strong drill motor with a half-inch chuck, and also the right size hole-saw for each different tube diameter. And, if you're making several notches, having a few back-up hole-saws is a must, as they tend to dull out. Also, a notch made by hole-saw might give you a nice even radius, however, the edges will still need to be deburred. In the acceptable category, a manual hand-notcher probably offers the best and cleanest results, but with this tool, even with good leverage, you better have some muscle in your arms!

A well-equipped shop that regularly fabricates with tubing, either round or square, should have a precision notcher such as the Scotchman GN6DE. Scotchman has several models to choose from, both with and without a dust extraction feature.

The Scotchman GN6DE is the company's top-of-the-line grit notcher. It features a 5-horsepower motor that turns a 6-inch by 78.75-inch belt at 2,950rpm. This model has a maximum notch capability of 5.5 inches O.D. at 90 degrees, and 4.0 inches O.D. at 45 degrees. Minimum notch size is .75 inches. Most importantly, the Scotchman is an extremely versatile and easy-to-use machine.

The tube is secured in the sliding clamp on the Scotchman machine and the end can be notched to the correct angle as you pull the feed lever which slides the fixture toward the gring belt.

It looks like it might fit, but we won't know until we try it with a valve cover.

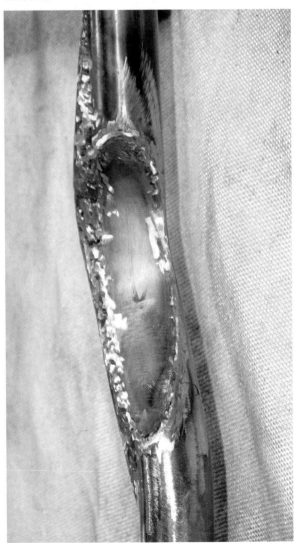

Once welded and formed, the tubes can be hit with a DA sander and some 36-grit paper, then the frame will be ready to start the molding.

After the tube is welded up it is ground down for looks and ready to hit the body shop.

The engine now shows how tight it is in the custom made frame. It's little touches like this that take special care.

A bit of grinding and deburring at the rear of the frame tubes and we were ready to test the tail lights for fit and function.

the tubing have a flush fit all around where it connects to another tube. Having to fill large gaps with weld will increase the amount of heat generated on the metal and make the joint weaker.

Engine, Transmission and Axle Mounts

Before I could come up with the final design for the top tubes, I needed to start mocking up the lower tubes with the engine in place. Although I trust my initial measurements with the tape measure, things have a way of coming together just a little different from the plan. So, with the lower portion of the frame completed up to the rear section, it was time to put the engine in place to determine the location of the mounts and the exact contour of the top tubes. The stacked array of superchargers would also have to be placed on top of the engine because I wanted the frame to wrap around the assembly as tight as possible.

Now the one thing that I was not looking forward to was hoisting a big-block Chevy engine up onto the welding table and maneuvering it around to fabricate mounts and

We measured twice, cut once, welded carefully, and the result was a perfect alignment of all the parts.

And this is how Bruce wound up with an axle in his eye... not really, but it could have happened! Brian is trying another test for fit between welds. The process of welding is one that frequently warps and tweaks metal into all kinds of positions and you will have to perform frequent checks to make sure that all your parts still fit together as you weld.

design the top portion of the frame. But the time was here, so I looked into the possibility of using a lightweight foam replica of the engine to ease this part of the fabrication. Fortunately, I recalled seeing just a product displayed at the last Specialty Equipment Market Association (SEMA) show that I attended. The company was called P-Ayr and I immediately put a call in to them. My main concern was that if I chose to use a foam engine block for the mock-up of the frame and all the mounts, would it be accurate? Well, P-Ayr responded instantly by delivering one of their high-density foam blocks and, at first glance, I thought it was the real thing. The amount of detail in their replica was true to factory GM spec, right down to the Chevy orange paint. Now, I was ready to build a frame!

I also received another shipment that I needed before I could continue. This one was from Holley Performance Products and it contained the big-block intake manifold for the Weiand/Holley superchargers that would top the block off. For me, waiting for parts seems to take longer than the process of installing them. With the P-Ayr block and Holley induction system in place, we were able to design

a set of motor mounts and continue the frame fabrication from the neck piece all the way to the rear axle.

At least that was the order in which it should have gone but, unfortunately, it didn't. While waiting for the mock-up block and manifold to arrive, I got a little impatient and used my rough dimensions to fabricate most of the tubes and even started welding some of them together. The reason I did this was not all due to impatience; we were filming a segment out in the shop for an upcoming build show and the production crew needed to shoot the work on the frame. I gave them the footage that they wanted and all I could do was hope for the best for the layout of the frame.

Well, as luck would have it, once we had the foam block in place and tried to put the blowers onto the manifold, we hit our first roadblock. The supercharger belt drive hit the front part of the frame and the bottom cradle section of the frame looked a bit too narrow at the starter and oil filter area. This just happened to be the area where I placed the frame splices and where the vertical braces meet the lower frame rails.

The Mock-Up Block

Brian brings the engine for a trial fit. No, he's not freakishly strong; this engine block is made of sturdy urethane foam and weighs in at a mere 24 lbs.

The P-Ayr foam engine block is an accurate full-size replica of the cast-iron Chevy block complete with threaded inserts in all the right places made especially for mock-up jobs such as this. The bare foam block weighs in at just 24 lbs. on our shop scale, much easier to lift and maneuver about than a 250-lb. cast-iron block! P-Ayr makes foam block replicas for all popular automotive and motorcycle engines as well as transmissions, water pumps, superchargers, manifolds and other accessories.

We put the P-Ayr foam block to the test by fabricating all of our engine and transmission mounts with it and found that every mounting bolt for our real engine and trans was a perfect fit. This mock-up engine block was one of the key components that allowed us to fabricate the Chopper One frame so quickly and easily. Knowing that we could remove and install the mock-up block during fabrication without a cumbersome engine hoist to deal with gave us the incentive to do so several times. The result was a frame that hugs the engine with precision tolerances with some clearances as tight as an eighth of an inch!

I expected the most labor-intensive part of this frame build to be the repeated installation and removal of the big 502 engine each time we were checking the fit of a tube. The solution came from P-Ayr Products—the company that "builds engines that don't run." Made of lightweight urethane and exact in all dimensions, the mock-up engine block solved the problem of having to fit several hundred pounds of real engine into the bike during fabrication of the frame.

The P-Ayr Products mockup block has threaded inserts that allow you to add engine parts, brackets and accessories to the block for fitting a complete engine into a frame.

The engine was set back about 5 inches to create space for the blower drive and belts. This moved the engine closer to the rear tire and allowed me to stick close to the stock wheelbase length of 82 inches.

The first time I assembled the engine it was a bit overwhelming. This was, indeed, an extreme chopper build!

Had we used a cast-iron block for fabricating the frame, we naturally would've minimized the number of times that we had to remove and replace the block, so the final fit would probably not have been as precise as it was.

The real engine would only be installed after the frame was complete and painted, and with the split frame design, we would actually be installing the frame around the engine rather than the engine into the frame.

Even though we did not need the superchargers at this point we added them for fun and to give us a sneak peek of things to come.

A Splice That's Twice as Nice

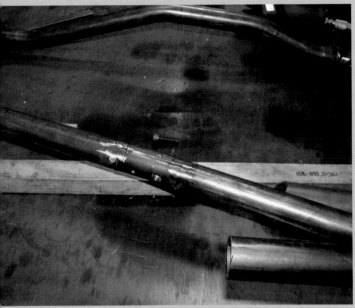

The splice that I originally designed for stunt car roll cages worked perfectly for the Chopper One frame. It is virtually undetectable, except for the counter sunk Allen bolt heads.

Due to the size of their power plants, Boss Hoss frames are two-piece designs. The frame for Chopper One would be no different. However, the splices that I used were my own design. These have a hardened ball bearing mounted between the two bolts that serve to lock the splice together.

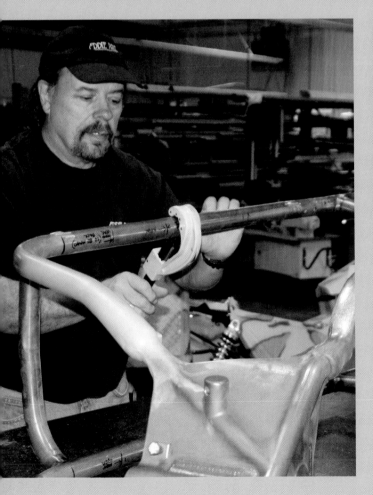

No sooner had I put them in than I noticed the starter and oil filter were too close to the frame and the whole section had to be moved outward. A tubing cutter (at left) was employed to cut the frame with the least amount of collateral damage.

Inventing on the fly is something that has sort of become second nature for me. Regardless of what type of fabrication or modification I might be doing, I always seem to try to come up with a tool or a method to make the task easier or better. Case in point: As soon as I got into disassembling the stock Boss Hoss frame, I took one look at how the frame was spliced and

Once the tubes were cut for the splices, the frame was set on the welding table while the new sections of tubing were being fabricated. Our table is topped with a specially milled flat sheet of 1/2-inch cold-rolled steel that we can use for setting and taking measurments on jobs such as this.

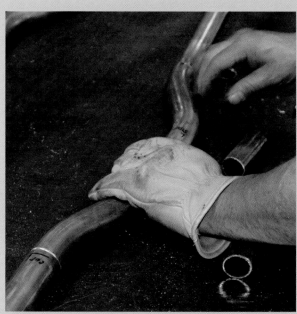

The bowed-out sections were neatly grafted into place. A short length of smaller-diameter tubing was inserted where the tubes joined to add reinforcement. Whenever a frame tube must be modified in this way, the joint needs to be stronger than the original tube when you are done with a job.

The mid down tubes are cut and re-angled slightly for a tighter fit around the transmission and an extra section of tube is added inside the splice for strength. This is a minor modification, but it is the details like this that will make the bike stand out at a show.

immediately devised a cleaner and stronger splice right there on the spot. This isn't to say that the factory splice is not strong, it is, but there is a difference.

The frame splice that I used on the Chopper One frame is actually a product that I manufacture and use for roll cage constructions. Since many of the cages that I make are full cages for stunt vehicles, the tube configurations can be quite complex, and getting

into a stunt car sometimes requires the flexibility of a contortionist. To facilitate entry into a stunt car, I designed a special splice for the side brace tubes that made them easily removable without sacrificing any strength. I simply adapted the idea to the custom Chopper One frame by scaling down the diameter of the splice from 2 inches to 1.5 inches.

The four Boss Hoss splices were made out of a solid

Each tube in the splice is then MIG welded up and ground down for molding of the frame.

This is a close-up of a typical splice in the frame with the inner (smaller) tube welded in place and a gap (intentional to allow the weld to be below the surface of the tube. This area will be welded up until the tube is the same diameter as the original tube. It can then be ground down for a "metal finish."

The motor mount is welded up out of tubing and plate steel.

The front down-tube cross brace is made of the same size tubing as the frame and will give a lot more strength to the structure once welded into place.

bar of cold rolled steel, with the diameter turned down at one end enough to fit about an inch into the connecting tube. The other connecting end was milled halfway through the tube to become a splice, so when two of these splices are rotated 180 degrees, they can be joined. To secure the splice together, two holes were drilled in the milled section, allowing the two parts to be bolted together. Now, what we do that Boss Hoss does not do is to mill a 1/2-inch half-round recess between the two bolts on each splice and insert a 1/2-inch steel ball bearing between the two bolts.

With a precision fit into the half-round recess, the steel ball serves two purposes: one is to help align the two splices during assembly, and the other is to add strength. The locking ball adds a lot more strength to the shear factor as the splice will now have to shear a 1/2-inch steel bearing in half to break loose. Without the locking ball, the splice is only as strong as the bolts holding it together.

The tail lights were turned on a lathe from a solid bar of translucent red plastic. The inside of the plastic was hollowed for better light transmission. The lenses were also turned to fit inside the frame tubing and held in place with a dab of adhesive.

The solution? Pull a few more feet of 1.5-inch tubing off the rack along with a couple of new splices and re-fabricate the lower section of the frame. Of course, if you happen to catch this build on television, you won't see this part of it because it was totally off camera. The slight modification that had to be made actually worked in my favor. I was able to eliminate the vertical support tubes under the seat area that were part of the original design in favor of a one-piece sweeping design that gave me the added clearance and looked better without compromising any strength. Now the motor mounts could be designed and welded into place along with the mounts for the transmission and rear axle.

As the frame tubes were aligned before welding, all clearances around the engine and transmission, as well as the axle area and front forks, were double-checked. A motorcycle frame is not exactly a square frame, so you will be dealing with a lot of angles as well as bend radiuses. It will tax your skill as a fabricator and tube bender, but the final results will reward you with an education in three-dimensional geometry. After fabricating a motorcycle frame, it won't take long for you to start thinking in angles and radiuses, and the whole process of bending will become second nature to you. I've built so many frames and roll cages that I can calculate in my head where a tube will wind up and about how long it should be to make a finished run

I credit much of my experience and know-how with tube fabrication to my early days when I used to manufacture

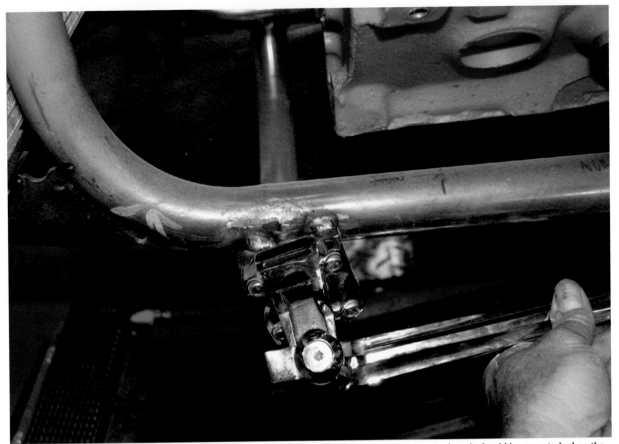

The kick stand was next and a special problem in itself, due in part to the fact that you need to know where it should be mounted when the bike is on the stand, and you also need to know where the kick stand should wind up when it is in the up position.

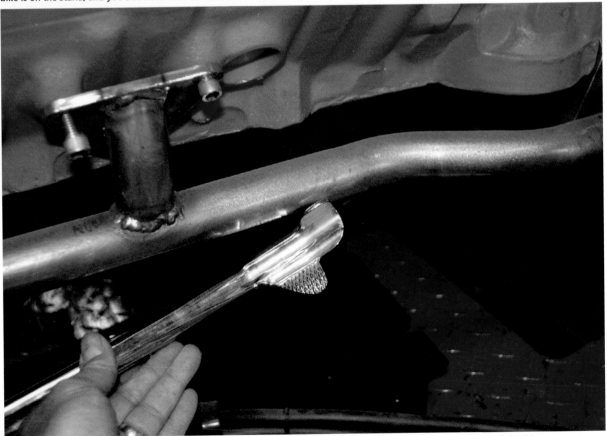

This is where the kick stand hits the frame and where we should add an extension with a rubber bumper. The kickstand should rotate past center so it will stay down when the bike's weight is on the stand, so this angle would not work and had to be changed later.

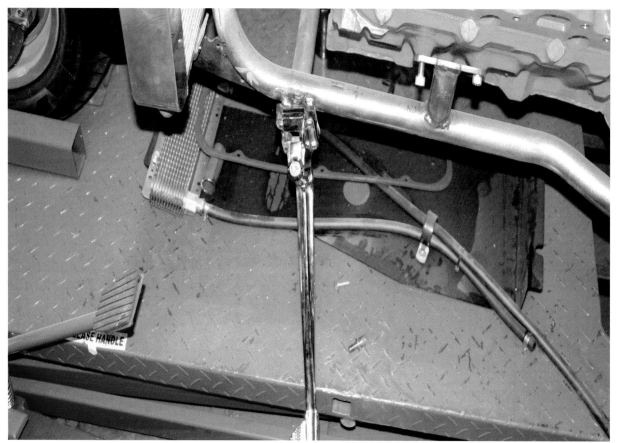

The stand was tested and did not extend forward enough, so I modified it by changing the top stop plate to a stainless steel design that allowed the stand to swing farther forward.

custom hang-gliders and, more recently, the big mechanical sharks, shark cages and submarines that I made for the Cousteau documentaries on great white sharks. Now, the process of fabricating a typical motorcycle frame seems relatively simple.

The top section of the frame is a bit more complicated than the down tubes and bottom rails. If you've ever had the chance to sit on a Boss Hoss, you probably noticed how wide the bike feels as you straddle it. For this reason, I wanted to kick the top tubes in at the seat area to provide a more comfortable feel, which meant a bunch of 20-degree bends both in and out with a 17-degree rotation to the right and another 20-degree rotation upwards. Well, again you get the idea. I also needed to add four frame splices to the two top tubes and bottom rails that would allow me to separate the new frame into two halves. Welding the splices in place before making any bends wasn't an option because the complication factor would have multiplied even more than it is. But splices were an absolute necessity if I wanted to be able to install or remove the big rat engine and transmission.

As Brian and I began to mock up the frame tubes on the welding table, I almost regretted not building a jig for this process. Almost! The tubes were a bit difficult to hold in place without the use of several clamps, but we managed to struggle through the mock up, alignment and welding of the entire frame without any special tools or fixtures.

The last thing I had to address was the kickstand. I decided to use the factory Boss Hoss kickstand, but mount it forward of its normal location on the lower down tube. The frame was now complete with the exception of the mounts for the fuel tank. Since Chopper One would be getting a totally new custom tank, we would have to wait until after the sheet metal fabrication was completed to add the last mounts to the frame.

At this point, it was time to do a little work on that big engine.

Chapter Three

The Drive Train—502 Cubic Inches of Big-Block Chevy!

The stock 502 was stripped down and the new supercharger was tested for fit and location of the bolts and ports.

According to the handy built-in dictionary on my computer, one of the definitions for the word "ultimate" is greatest. So if Chopper One was to become the ultimate custom bike, then the engine would have to follow suit. With the popularity of the Boss Hoss motorcycle rapidly rising, so too are the custom treatments by individual owners all across the country. A custom paint job on these V-8 machines seems to be standard fare, and more and more riders are starting to divert their attention to the drive train.

In a car, the drive train would be the driveshaft and differential, or rear end. The motorcycle equivalent to the driveshaft and rear end is a chain or a belt that links the transmission to a gear or pulley mounted to the rear wheel. Much thought must be put into the selection of individual drive train parts, because the end result determines the drivability, reliability and performance potential of the vehicle. In most cases, these three qualities—drivability, reliability and performance—are a well-balanced package from the factory. However, when any part of the drive train is modified, there is almost always a compromise involved.

The Boss Hoss factory drive train consists of two over-the-counter GM engine options: the 350-cubic-inch ZZ4 rated at 355 horsepower, and the 502-cubic-inch ZZ502 rated at 502 horses. Either of these two power plants are excellent choices in stock trim or as a starting point for engine modifications. In most cases, the normal output of 355 or 502 hp would be more than enough for anything on two wheels. But Chopper One needed more

Putting two blowers on top of a big block would be a tall order.

than the average V-8 bike (if there is such a thing!), and the transmission had to be strong enough to back it up. Due to the special construction of the Boss Hoss, the choice of transmissions is limited to the Boss Hoss two-speed automatic with reverse. Although we were putting a considerable increase in horsepower through the trans,

The Drive Train—502 Cubic Inches of Big-Block Chevy!

The exhaust ports were cleaned and scraped to remove a leftover gasket from the last gasket install.

The new intake gaskets were added in preparation for the final install of the supercharger manifold. We cover the engine with plastic bags each time we walk away from it so nothing gets in the crankcase.

This is the Dominator carb I would be using on the monster. It would get toned down a bit for the street, but this little setup will really drink the gas.

there seemed to be no issues of strength or longevity so far. If this were a car, the trans would connect to a driveshaft via heavy-duty universal joints to a beefy rear end. Chopper One will use a Gates Polychain belt to turn the rear wheel.

Or so it would appear, but to get from point "A" to point "B" we have a lot of work to do and a bit of "back-of-the-napkin" engineering to perform in order for all the components and hardware to fit and perform their respective duties. This is what separates the men from the boys in custom bike or car building. We (meaning my crew and me), are well aware of the fact that "things" do not always fit "other things" perfectly, or at all, for that

Here is the engine in the bike as the sheet metal work starts taking shape. We needed the engine in the bike to fit the tank around it.

The Dominatior is topped off with a scoop that will channel the air down the Dominator's throat to be mixed with gas and nitrous for pavement pounding power.

matter. So, when this happens, we normally plow ahead, expecting to cut, bend, stretch, weld, modify, customize, fabricate and design almost every part of the motorcycle as we go along. We often find ourselves in utter disbelief when something does fit as it should.

I think the big difference between an average mechanic and a custom fabricator is that the custom guy expects and lives for the challenge of things not fitting "out of the box" and derives pleasure in making it work. These are things that the average mechanic dreads. When things don't fit, the project will collect dust in a corner of his dark and dingy garage until he can motivate himself to work it out.

The engine was fitted with the superchargers just before putting the engine in the bike. Then the superchargers were removed so the weight and size would be at a minimum for fitting it into the frame. The fit was very close.

It was important to get the angles right at the top of the mid-manifold plate so that the top supercharger would sit parallel to the bottom one.

If you're thinking of becoming a custom fabricator or customizer, it is best to realize that every project will start off on a long and bumpy road, but when it's complete and if it's done right, the modifications should be so clean that the finished job might not even look modified at all. Only you will have the satisfaction and pride in saying "yes, I built that." The you can ramble on for hours about how you made this part fit that part and how you modified this so that it would clear that and you can wax on into the night as long as you have an interested audience. The satisfaction is well worth the effort, so keep this in mind as you work into the night on that design that you need to get out of your head and onto the road. Mine was Chopper One.

The GM ZZ502 "Crate" Engine

I'll start by describing the Chopper One drive train components and modifications, working from the engine back toward the rear tire. The engine is the heart of the bike but it is also separate from the frame and therefore can be worked on away from the frame as long as we have a good "stand-in" (studio talk), which we did. In most build-ups, the frame is mocked up using the actual engine. Because of the sheer size and weight of the Chevy engine, we used the P-Ayr big-block Chevy urethane foam block for the fabrication of the frame tubes, motor mounts and transmission mounts. The Boss Hoss engine was removed from the frame and bolted to one of the good solid engine

Belts were purchased that would be long enough to reach both pulleys and have just a bit of slack for adjustments, but not too much or the belt would not grab enough of the pulley diameter.

Once finished, the top supercharger stuck out of the tank opening as if it were mounted on the top of the tank. As they say "if you got it, flaunt it!"

The top splices of Chopper One's two-piece frame are evident in this photo. Once the tank is installed, the hairline seams are virtually undetectable.

In some areas of the frame your finger won't even fit through the gap. All the fine tuning and re-doing was well worth the effort to get a fit like this.

The Drive Train—502 Cubic Inches of Big-Block Chevy!

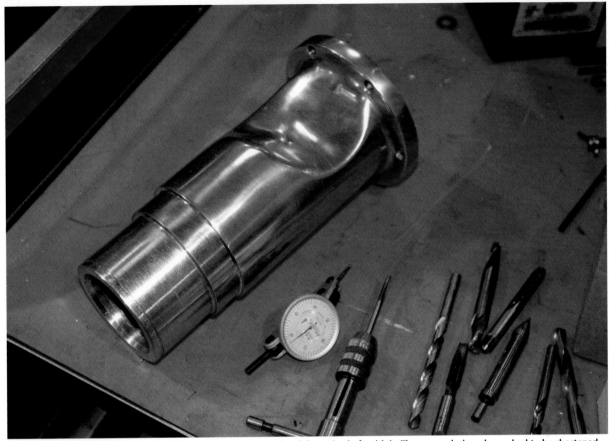

The short nose that houses the main shaft needed to be removed and the main shaft with it. The new redesigned nose had to be shortened to fit the shortened nose, but that was just a matter of cutting it and rethreading it and adding a keyway. Almost any machine shop can do this for you on a lathe.

The new top supercharger nose only took a few hours to make and all we did was remove about 6 inches from it and the main shaft. The nose was made from 6061-T6 aluminum bar.

stands that we picked up from Eastwood tools. This allowed us the ability to move it around the shop while we performed the modifications to the induction and exhaust systems.

By motorcycle standards, the "small" 350-cubic-inch Boss Hoss is huge! A stock late-model Harley-Davidson engine is 88 cubic-inches with a 145-cubic-inch stroker on the big end of the scale. So when you compare that to 502 cubes (or 8200cc's for you metric guys), the difference is pretty ridiculous! And the ZZ502 is the engine we are working with, but first we'll go over a few vital statistics on the stock bike.

The ZZ502 is available through GM Performance Parts as a short-block (minus heads), long-block (with heads) or fully assembled with heads, intake manifold, starter, and ignition system. The big-block is factory-rated at a whopping 502 ponies at 5200 rpm with a monstrous 567 lbs.-ft. of torque at 4200 rpm. The GM Gen VI cast-iron block has four-bolt main caps helping to keep the rods in place as you twist the grip. The crankshaft is forged steel, rods are forged and shot-peened, and pistons are forged aluminum. Static compression ratio is 9.6:1, making this a very streetable engine that won't rattle apart on pump gas.

Helping to keep the top end weight to a minimum are the GM Performance Parts aluminum oval-port heads with 110cc chambers. Moving the air-fuel mixture in and out are 2.25-inch intake valves with 1.88-inch stainless valves on the exhaust activated by a hydraulic roller camshaft with .527-inch lift on the intake, .544 inch on the exhaust, and 224/234 degrees of duration at .050 inches. The GM induction system is a dual-plane intake that is port-matched to the heads topped by an 850cfm carburetor. Ignition is an HEI type.

All Boss Hoss bikes use a special semi-automatic

A new shortened nose piece for the top Weiland supercharger was fabricated from solid billet aluminum alloy on one of our ProTrak CNC lathes. The finished product looks like a factory piece.

transmission with two forward gears and a reverse. There is no clutch on this trans, but shifting from first to second is manual. The three-wheeled trike version, because of its configuration, uses a GM Turbo-Hydramatic three-speed automatic.

Dry weight of the stock 502 Boss Hoss is 1,300 lbs. Chopper One will tip the scale at about 950 lbs. with an identical wheelbase of 82 inches. We kept the same wheelbase by moving the engine back 5 inches and putting the rear of the transmission almost against the front of the rear tire. On the stock Boss Hoss, the rear of the transmission is about 5 inches further forward of this point due to the space required by the rear swing arm suspension. Since the Chopper One has a rigid frame with no rear suspension, I was able to move the engine back to gain the much-needed space at the front of the engine for the blower drive belts. Getting the power to the rear wheel is a Gates Polychain belt.

Forced Induction With Dual Superchargers

Internally, the Gen VI block contains all the right stuff to build a mild blower motor with. Although the compression might be a tad on the high side for supercharging, we had to keep in mind that the bike would not be seeing too much full-throttle operation—at least not enough to warrant a new set of pistons and a bottom-end tear-down. So with

The new nose slips into place and is bolted on just like the original. We even used the main shaft bearing from the original nose.

The Drive Train—502 Cubic Inches of Big-Block Chevy!

The stop bolt was added next. For this we needed a little help because the tensioner had to be rotated and held at the tensioned angle by one person as another person installed the stop bolt.

The large C-clip was added and the belt tensioner was in place on the new part.

a compression ratio of 9.6:1 and judicious selection of the drive ratio, running Chopper One on pump gas with dual superchargers was still feasible. The first thing to come off the engine and hit the recycle bin was the GM Performance dual-plane aluminum intake manifold and carburetor. The distributor was also removed and set aside for re-installation later. The chromed 4-into-1 exhaust headers and pipes came off and would be replaced with "zoomie"-style headers.

A supercharger, or blower, is basically a pump that increases the density of the air and fuel mixture in the combustion process through a form of positive displacement compression. This method of force-feeding the engine produces more power from the cylinders by the simple process of increasing input volume into a fixed cylinder volume. On a normally aspirated (non-supercharged) engine, the intake cycle pulls in a what is referred to as a swept volume of fuel and air by creating a vacuum in the cylinders. The carburetor or fuel injector meters a precise mixture of air and fuel through the intake manifold and valves into the cylinder for combustion. This process actually decreases the air density a bit since the vacuum of air tends to separate the single air molecules. This winds up creating a very low pressure in the venturi section of the carburetor, which, in turn, creates suction inside the carb that pulls fuel out of the bowl. Fuel is then mixed with the air to create a combustible mixture. This mixture, once compressed in the cylinder by the piston, is ignited by the spark plug. The result is rapid expansion from the heat that pushes the piston down the cylinder (path of least resistance), which turns the crankshaft.

When you want more power from an engine, you can cheat the four-cycle system using a few simple laws of physics. First, you can increase your compression ratio to compress the air/fuel mixture in the cylinder, or you can

With the tensioner in place, the assembly was ready for the top pulley to be added.

The base plate was made on a mill using a CNC program, but could just as easily have been cut out on a band saw.

Blowers: The "Roots" of Rotors and Lobes

A supercharger is simply an air pump, and air pumps fall into two basic categories: positive-displacement or centrifugal. A turbocharger is an exhaust-driven centrifugal pump, whereas a supercharger is an engine-driven positive-displacement pump. There are also centrifugal superchargers, however, I don't want to stray too far into unrelated territory. Since I would be installing not one but two superchargers on Chopper One, I'm also including a little background data for support.

Some of the different types of superchargers include: centrifugal, Roots-type (named after the designers of this pump, the Roots brothers), vane-type, screw-type, axial flow and the Wankel rotary. I am sure that I've overlooked a few, but the point is not all superchargers are the same. The familiar GMC supercharger that you often see coming through the hood of a street machine or rod is a Roots-type that uses two- or three-lobe rotors to pump air. Choices are numerous and the sizes are plenty that determine how many cubic inches of air you want to cram down through the intake valves.

The Sprintex twin-screw supercharger that I mentioned previously is a rotary compressor with two helical rotors that rotate in opposite directions. One rotor takes the form of the left-hand helix, the other the right-hand helix and the two mesh together to form chambers that push the air through to the engine. The rotors never touch, but are synchronized by a pair of gears operating in a lubricated chamber, which is separated from the rotor chamber. The reason that this type of supercharger is of a helical design is that if it were just a straight set of parallel lobes, you would get a pulsing of pressure, rather than a flow of pressure. With the helical design, one lobe is just starting its compression as the previous one is just ending. This generates a smoother flow of air and gas at all rpm. There are a number of different types of superchargers on the market, but they all perform the same task of forcing the air/fuel mixture into an engine.

The capacity of a supercharger is rated by the cubic-inch displacement per single revolution of the unit's rotors. So, a 142-cubic-inch supercharger displaces 142 cubic inches of air and fuel with each 360-degree rotation. The air/fuel mixture of a normally aspirated engine is also referred to as the air charge. Forcing this mixture into the engine essentially converts it into a super-air charge, hence the name "supercharger." This supercharged air/fuel mixture can reach or, in some engines, exceed 100 percent volumetric efficiency. Volumetric efficiency, without going into too much technical detail, is the total cylinder capacity of an engine as it relates to the volume of air/fuel mixture that is actually inducted. The pressure increase provided by a supercharger or turbocharger is referred to as boost pressure, or simply boost. Typical boost will range from about 6 to 8 lbs. per square inch (psi). Since normal air pressure at sea level is 14.7 psi, adding 6 or 8 psi to the 14.7 will increase the volume of air and gas in the cylinder by approximately 50 percent. Theoretically, this increase should translate into that much more horsepower, but remember that the horsepower required to drive the supercharger must be subtracted from this increase to provide the net total gain.

force more fuel and air through the carburetor thereby increasing the density of the mixture. Unlike the normally aspirated process that tends to lessen the pressure by pulling the air/fuel mixture into the engine, the supercharger effectively compresses the air/fuel mixture into the engine, increasing the density.

Another thing to keep in mind is that cooler air is denser than hot air. In relation to your engine, a cooler air charge will result in more horsepower. So when you drive in the fog on a cool night and your car seems to run much better than on a hot day, this is not your imagination. The engine runs better because the air is denser! Remember that higher temperature expands air and lower temperature condenses it. This is the operating theory behind those water injectors; cooler air equals denser air resulting in a slight but very real increase in power. Of course, nothing in this world comes free, and horsepower is no exception. It takes horsepower to drive a supercharger and that is power taken away from the rear wheel of your car, so you lose a little bit of power, but gain more than you lose, so the net gain is well worth it. Even turbochargers absorb some horsepower by creating a bit of backpressure on the exhaust of your engine forcing your engine to crank out more pressure to spin the turbo thus stealing power from the back end of your engine.

In the world of hot rodding, no other engine has seen the working end of a wrench as much as the venerable Chevy V-8. It is the most popular engine on the receiving end of high-performance tuning. This fact put me in somewhat of a dilemma when it came time to power-tune the engine for Chopper One. What could I do to the Chopper One

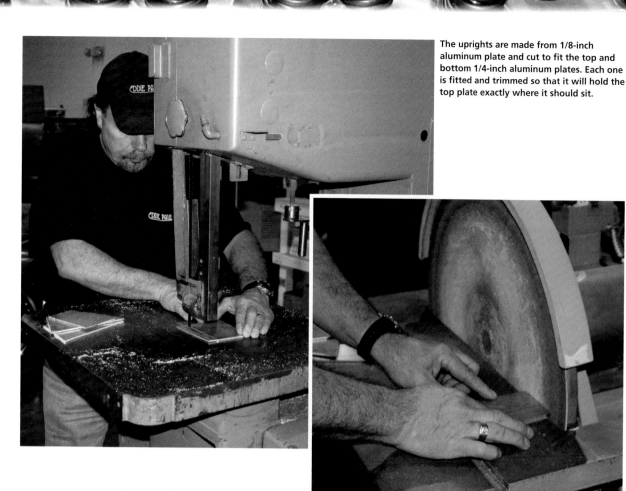

The uprights are made from 1/8-inch aluminum plate and cut to fit the top and bottom 1/4-inch aluminum plates. Each one is fitted and trimmed so that it will hold the top plate exactly where it should sit.

The edges of each part can be cleaned up and trimmed to perfection with a large disc sander. Whichever side of the sander is used, the disc should be spinning downward onto the part.

engine that hasn't already been done before? Well, the answer that I came up with would both solve my dilemma as well as help me fit things into the tight confines of the custom Chopper One frame tubes.

Superchargers on automotive engines have been around for more than a century, and various configurations of multiple superchargers date almost as far back. After all, if one is good, two must be better, right? Well, the idea of stacking two superchargers seems to me to be a relatively simple concept, but after researching the subject, I was surprised that I could not find much info. In fact, I couldn't even find a single article or photo in my vast library of books and magazines that showed an example of two vertically stacked superchargers. I came across a few notable examples of engines with multiple superchargers, but the configuration was either in tandem or parallel; not stacked or in succession. Aston-Martin's Vantage LeMans V600 was twin-supercharged and produced a whopping 600 hp out of its 5.3-liter V8. I also found a few drag boats, such as Livorsi's MerCruiser-powered Virage, that sported twin superchargers. I even found one guy that put a Chevy 350 into a Porsche 914 and added two Sprintex superchargers. But I couldn't find anything on engines with two stacked Roots-type blowers.

An exotic induction system is almost always the focal point of a high-performance engine. The more elaborate the system is, the more impressive the overall engine is. Because of the abundance of performance-related add-ons available for the Chevy engine, Boss Hoss owners have a virtually limitless selection of bolt-on horsepower to choose from. Upgrades from the stock GM Performance Parts aluminum intake can range from a simple swap to a higher performing aftermarket manifold to a forced induction system such as a supercharger, turbocharger, nitrous oxide injection, or a combination of any or all of these. I've already seen dual-quad tunnel ram setups and single blowers protruding through custom Boss Hoss fuel tanks, but it seems that nobody has yet gone to a multiple blower system.

Although a supercharger is still considered an exotic form of induction, it is also a fairly simple bolt-on item that is available in kit form from companies such as Weiand. Unfortunately, doubling the superchargers as I planned to do on Chopper One is not as easy as it sounds. There is no kit available for adding a second blower to the first one, and not many examples to refer to that would give me even a little bit of guidance on how to do this. So, how do you add two superchargers to the engine? And why?

The edges are sanded for straightness and rechecked for fit. Once they are perfect they can be clamped together and welded.

The assembly is then welded up and set aside to be installed after the bike is painted. You can see the O-ring grooves that have been milled in the top plate. This is just one way to seal the mid-manifold plate; the other is to just use a flat gasket. We prefer O-rings.

The outer holes are drilled and tapped to accept the four threaded rods that extend up through the top supercharger. We used stainless steel for all the hardware on the bike.

Well, the answer to the latter is easy. Installing a single supercharger, even a big 6-71 GMC blower, on a Boss Hoss is no groundbreaking feat. Also, a single blower, although impressive, just wouldn't provide the visual impact that I needed for this project. I wanted something totally outrageous—something that even a hard-core power freak would not even consider doing on any engine. But it had to be feasable from an engineering standpoint and still not require us to alter the frame or fuel tank any more than we had to. These general parameters led me to the type of

The two superchargers are stacked and the bolt length measured and cut to exact length. It's easier to do this on a bench than on the bike.

superchargers I would need to use and the configuration that I would have to place them in.

Once I had the idea of running dual superchargers on Chopper One, practicality and even sanity seemed to take a back seat to whatever I could do to bolster the bike's aesthetic shock value! Arranging dual superchargers in anything other than a stacked array was not an option since I did not want any part of the induction system expanding outside (to the left and right) of the frame. The width of a GMC 6-71-style blower would consume all of the usable space for a fuel tank, so the most practical choice for a pair of huffers would be two of Holley Performance Products Weiand 177 Pro-Street Superchargers for Chevy big-block oval-port heads. Weiand offers a wide range of

superchargers from 142 to 8-71.

Of course, Weiand or any other aftermarket manufacturer for that matter, does not make a blower-to-blower adaptor that would allow me to bolt one supercharger on top of another. From a fabricator's perspective, the solution was a fairly simple one: I would design and make my own. In addition to mating the two blowers together, another critical modification that would have to be made was in the drive assembly, but before I could accurately determine what changes, if any, would be required in the nose assemblies, I needed to get both housings mounted in place.

Since the cylinder heads, intake manifold and Weiand superchargers are all aluminum, fabricating the blower-to-blower adaptor from any other material would look out

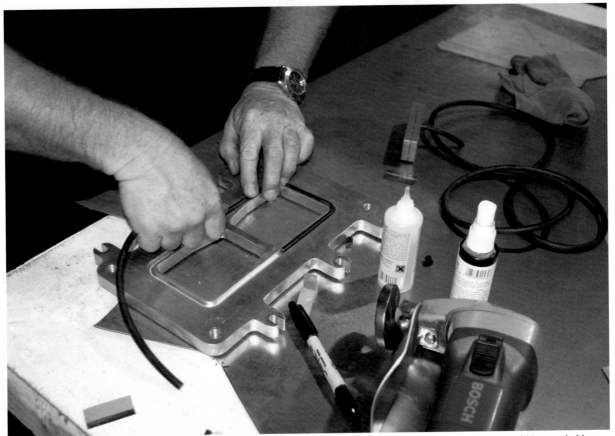

All you need to make an O-ring is a single-edge razor blade and some super glue (Cyanoacrylate). I like the Slo-Zap CA sold in most hobby shops, and if you are as impatient as me a small bottle of Zip Kicker (accelerator for the super glue). I found out you can order O-ring stock on spools of 10 to100 feet in whatever diameter you like.

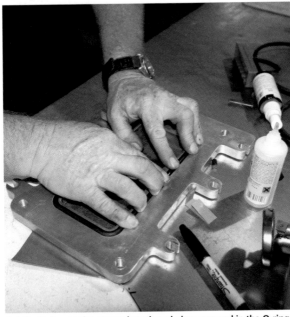

Cut the O-ring to the proper length and place one end in the O-ring groove, then put a small amount of super glue on the other cut end of the O-ring stock and press the two ends together in the O-ring groove. This will insure proper alignment of the ends. Without accelerator it will take a few minutes to set; with the accelerator it will take a few seconds. Do not use too much glue or it will not set.

of place. Furthermore, aluminum would be the easiest material to work with. I started out by selecting a few choice pieces of 6061-T6 aluminum alloy from my shop's scrap metal bin. The adaptor plate would actually consist of two plates, an upper and lower, with a large open plenum in between. One of the benefits of forced induction with a supercharger is that the entire system up to the intake valves is pressurized with the air/fuel mixture; there is no longer a flow that requires tuned runners or porting. Supercharging overcomes inefficiencies in these areas. Therefore, the design of the adaptor plenum is not at all critical as long as it does not restrict the flow. To avoid restriction, I made sure that the adaptor plenum maintained the same inside diameter as that of the supercharger's mounting flanges.

The first piece that I made was the base plate for the top of the bottom supercharger. To insure adequate sealing between the blowers and the adaptor, both the top and bottom plate would be O-ringed. The bottom plate would be nothing more than a carburetor base plate with a standard Holley four-barrel bolt pattern. It was a simple matter of copying the carburetor gasket pattern onto a piece of half-inch aluminum plate. I took advantage of having a CNC machine shop and had the plate milled, but it could easily be cut to shape with a band saw or even a saber saw. Grooving the plate for the O-ring was definitely a job best performed on a mill. This O-ring groove will have to be cut on the blower side of the plate only, and this is the plate that will mount to the lower supercharger.

Eddie Paul's Extreme Chopper Building

If you look closely you can see the seam, but if done correctly the seam is just as strong as the rest of the O-ring.

To measure the length, simply push the O-ring into the groove and let it overlap. That is the cutting point.

Keep in mind that an O-ring must seal all the way around. A simple and inexpensive trick here is to make a pattern out of clear plastic just to visually check the sealing surface before cutting the O-ring groove in the metal. This plastic pattern can then be taken to a machine shop to be used by the machinist for setting up the mill.

Next, I made the top plate for the adaptor. At this point, I knew from past experience that even something as simple as fabricating this adaptor could lead to problems if I didn't keep the individual pieces organized and clearly marked. What I like to do is identify each part using a felt-tip marker. I clearly indicated each part with a name or number designation and also made some reference marks to show its orientation (inner side, outer side, top edge,

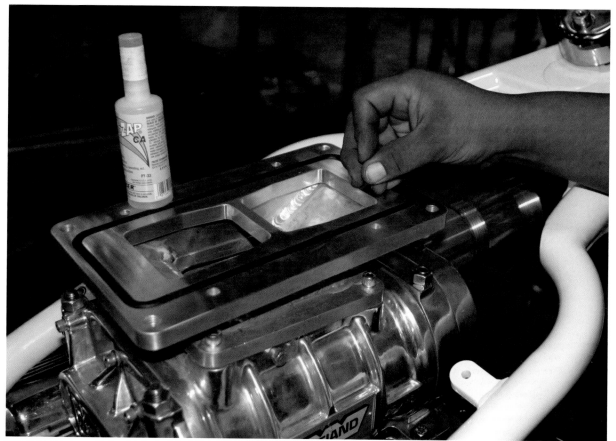

It's not hard to be an O-ring fabricator! And there are not many of them around.

An O-ring splicing tool is a handy little gadget that will insure a perpendicular cut on the O-ring.

bottom edge, etc.) with the other pieces of the assembly. This is especially helpful if somebody other than yourself will be performing the final welding of the pieces, or if you tend to be a little forgetful.

When it comes to fabrication of parts like an adaptor plate, you'll find that there are various levels of precision required, depending on the application. As you can see in the photos, the confined space within the Chopper One frame leaves very little room for error. Not only must the adaptor plenum adapt to two very different diameters, but the mounting holes for the two blower housings must vertically line up to insure that the drive assemblies are parallel with each other. Other important factors to consider are access to the adaptor's mounting hardware, and clearance of the entire induction system around the frame and tank. The height of the adaptor would determine the spacing between the two Weiand superchargers and I tried to keep this to a minimum for several reasons.

At a minimum height, the adaptor would put the Weiand scoop directly in front of my face when I sit on the bike. Normally, this would be a bad thing, but because I planned to modify the scoop to eliminate the obstruction, it was now mandatory that the adaptor plate be a specific height. With the upper and lower plates made of half-inch aluminum alloy, it was time to fabricate the plenum chamber. For this particular adaptor, the "plenum chamber" would be nothing more than a four-sided rectangle that would connect the two plates together. The height of the plenum chamber will determine the overall height of the system so, again, meticulous measurements were necessary.

Structural integrity of the adaptor plate is a fairly critical issue—not so much for its mounting strength as its ability to contain the pressure. If the chamber was an even rectangle, it could be machined from billet or formed from a single sheet of aluminum. But this rectangle starts as a square from

the Holley plate pattern and must "adapt" to the relatively larger opening underneath the top blower. Its sole purpose is to contain and direct the air/fuel mixture to the next supercharger. A leak in any part of the adaptor plate, even a very minor one, could be potentially disastrous, especially when firing up the engine for the first time. Venting the fuel mix to the atmosphere under pressure accompanied by an unexpected backfire could lead to an engine fire at least, or shrapnel from an exploded adaptor.

With the top and bottom plates made, I took careful measurements of the space between the superchargers. I found that if I wanted to have the top supercharger on a parallel horizontal plane with the bottom one, the adaptor would have to have a slight rise from rear to front. This was to compensate for the angle of the Weiand 177's carburetor mounting surface. Since the front of most vehicles tends to lift upon hard acceleration, the carburetor sits with a downward tilt at the front so that as the front of the vehicle lifts, the floats in the carb remain level. I took into account the total thickness of the two plates (1 inch) and found that the height of the plenum would be 1 inch at the rear and 2 inches at the front. I cut the four sides out of plastic first and taped them together so that I could check the spacing. When I was satisfied that everything would fit and line up, I untaped the plastic pieces to use them as templates for cutting them out of metal. Once the pieces were cut, the top and bottom plate and all four sides of the plenum chamber were TIG welded with our Esab Heliarc 252 welder.

Once the blower-to-blower adaptor was completed and tested for leaks (see sidebar), I set it aside for assembly after the paint job.

Nitrous anyone?

In most cases, the addition of a supercharger provides more than enough of a performance boost to satisfy the need for speed. But if you haven't guessed by now, I was after extreme visual impact and overkill with Chopper One! So the only thing left to do at this point was to top off the two Weiand superchargers with a killer nitrous system. In essence, nitrous oxide injection serves the exact same purpose as a supercharger, which is why a lot of people refer to it as a supercharger in a bottle.

The chemical symbol for nitrous oxide is N2O, for two nitrogen atoms and one oxygen atom. A nitrous injector is perhaps the most common power bolt-on among today's performance enthusiasts. Most kits from companies such as Nitrous Oxide Systems (N.O.S.) are easy to install. The system that I chose to install on Chopper One, however, was a little more complex due to the amount of boost that it is capable of.

Nitrous oxide is a non-flammable gas that serves as an oxidizer when injected into the air/fuel mixture. In a nutshell, when more oxygen is inducted into the mixture, the engine is capable of burning more fuel. A nitrous kit provides you with a balanced system to inject nitrous oxide

"How Do You See the Road?!"

Throughout the entire construction of Chopper One and after it was finished, this was the first thing that each and every person who saw the bike asked me! Why? Well, I guess it's because the Weiand air scoop and Holley Dominator carburetor sits directly in front of the rider's face!

While fabricating the blower-to-blower adaptor, visibility of the road from the rider's position was my primary concern. When I first mocked up the blowers on the P-Ayr foam block in the frame and straddled the bike about where I would be seated when riding, I could tell that once the carburetor and filter where installed, I'd have a good view of my induction system and little else. But this is, after all, an "extreme" chopper build, so I considered this a small price to pay for the bike to look the part.

Sometimes, the best ideas and unique designs come about either by accident, sheer luck, or, in this case, from just kidding around. When I mocked up the superchargers with the carburetor and scoop on the unfinished Chopper One and assumed a riding position, the scoop was less than 12 inches in front of my face. One of the guys in the shop said, "Hey, you're gonna need a little windshield on that thing!" It was a joke,

I kept hearing "how do you see over the air scoop?" The simplest way to solve the problem was to add a windshield to the back of the scoop, which in itself became a novelty.

but the idea instantly stuck in my head. Chopper One would have the world's smallest windshield when it was done.

with the proper amount of additional fuel to prevent an excessively lean mixture from entering the combustion chamber. The number one cause of engine failure when nitrous oxide is involved is not supplementing the oxygen boost with an adequate amount of additional fuel. And, arguably, the second most common cause of engine failure is when the injection system is engaged before the engine is under a full-throttle load. For most applications, I highly recommend the use of a nitrous oxide injection kit and following the instructions to avoid any problems.

The nitrous system for Chopper One is not available as a kit and is actually comprised of a custom-made nitrous injector plate along with N.O.S. tanks, fittings and hardware, and custom lines made by Earl's Supply. Although the actual power increase will vary from one engine to the next, this is a two-stage plate that can deliver

That little red anodized block under the Dominator is a two-stage nitrous block that adds an additional 350 hp to the already overburdened Chevy. That extra power will never be needed, but it was a simple addition.

Braided fuel and nitrous lines are the only way to go as they not only add a clean look, but the added strength of the stainless steel braiding will allow the rubber hose inside to withstand a much higher burst pressure than it would without the braiding.

The Drive Train—502 Cubic Inches of Big-Block Chevy!

Testing For Leaks

There is only one method that I use to test a fabrication such as an adaptor plate for leaks: a vacuum test plate.

A vacuum test plate is nothing more than a rigid plastic plate (polycarbonate works well as it is almost unbreakable) that, for this test, measures about 12 inches x 12 inches. The plate should be thick enough to avoid flexing under the pressure of vacuum, and a Schrader valve (tire valve) must be mounted in the center of it for attaching a vacuum pump. The test plate that I made to test the blower-to-blower adaptor measured a half-inch in thickness. Since there are two open sides to this adaptor, I also had to make a second plate to form an enclosure that could hold pressure. Both plates must seal to the adaptor as they would to the supercharger using rubber gasket material or an O-Ring. With the test plates attached to the adaptor, either a hand-operated vacuum pump such as a Mityvac with a gauge or an electric vacuum pump with a gauge is connected to the Schrader valve, and then a vacuum is pulled. The amount of vacuum does not have to be much; as little as 5 inches will be enough (Note: vacuum pressure is measured in inches of mercury, whereas positive air pressure, such as tire pressure, is measured in pounds per square inch, or psi.). Then the gauge is monitored for any drop in pressure. Of course, this is an oversimplification of the testing process, but it is not a very complicated procedure.

To test any structure, such as this adaptor or even a gas tank, for leaks requires just a few basic items.

Testing things such as a fuel tank can be done without having to make any kind of test plate at all. You simply need to make sure that the tank is sealed off at all openings and allow for a connector to attach to a vacuum hose. If gaskets or O-rings are involved, lubricating them with silicone grease will help to create an airtight seal.

To perform the actual test for leaks, you can draw a small amount of vacuum and simply monitor the gauge (most vacuum pumps have a gauge attached). Any measurable drop in pressure indicates a leak. Or you can get a little more high-tech. I prefer to draw a vacuum and then test for leaks with an ultrasonic sensor. An ultrasonic sensor is a handy little tool that can detect even the slightest sound, such as that which a very tiny air leak might make. The sensor can indicate a leak for you with an audible signal through a set of headphones, or with a visual signal by way of LED lights. My ultrasonic sensor has a row of LED lights; the greater the sound of the leak, the more lights that flash. A company called Amprobe makes a good affordable hand-held ultrasonic tester.

If the ultrasonic sensor detects the sound of an air leak, or if you notice a drop in pressure on the gauge, the next step is to pinpoint the exact source of the leak and repair it. Fortunately, the adaptor plate for Chopper One was leak-free.

---

a maximum boost of 100 horsepower with the first stage and 250 horsepower with the second stage for a total boost of 350 horsepower. A two-stage plate allows you to activate the injector at two different points during acceleration.

The Chopper One nitrous plate was made by Ron Hammel several years ago. Ron was one of the originators of nitrous oxide use in racing engines. His company was called 10,000RPM back in the '70s and '80s and it specialized in nitrous oxide injectors and racing clutches. Engine requirements for a system with this much boost are critical to avoid disaster. Not only must the nitrous system have an adequate supply of fuel, but also the lower end of the engine must be capable of withstanding the extreme power boost. A balanced forged steel crank, forged connecting rods and forged pistons are a must.

The Exhaust System

As the burnt gas will be leaving the engine at a high velocity at fluctuating frequency and varying pressure, the audible tone will be nothing short of a loud roar. Redirecting and slowing down the exhaust gas through

mufflers will lessen its volume to a streetable level, but once again, streetability was not my primary goal with this buildup. The redirection of exhaust gases is actually a very sophisticated method of creating what is known as "active noise cancellation." By design, a performance exhaust system is a series of tubes and chambers that allow the "reflected pressure" of the exhaust gas to equal the "exit-pressure" and thus cancel each other out, resulting in a net zero pressure—or as near to that as possible.

In terms of sound and decibels, that is roughly how a muffler works. All of this is irrelevant in this case, however, because Chopper One would not have mufflers. Instead, the exhaust will flow through a set of custom-made dragster-style tubes more commonly referred to as Zoomies. Because of the already excessive power-to-weight ratio of the Chopper One power plant, the performance efficiency of the exhaust system was of little concern. As long as the exhaust gas could exit, that's all that mattered!

To start with, I picked a diameter of pipe I wanted to use and that would look cool on the bike, and that was 1.25-inch outside diameter with a .120 wall, by about 24 inches

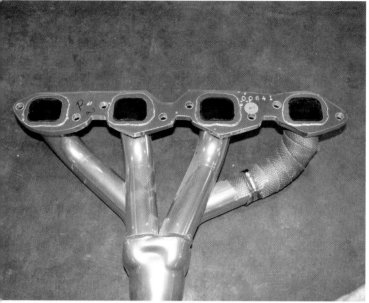

The stock Boss Hoss headers were removed and measured in order to duplicate a new set of Zoomies that I planned on fabricating out of 1/4-inch steel plate and .120-inch thick roll bar tubing.

The header flanges were then added to the foam block to check for fit. I found out that both sides were exactly the same so we only needed to make one drawing and machine two parts.

After the pipes were cut and bent and the ends miter cut we were ready to start tack welding each one into place.

When the angle was determined, the clamp on the cutoff saw was set and the rest of the pipes were cut at the same angle.

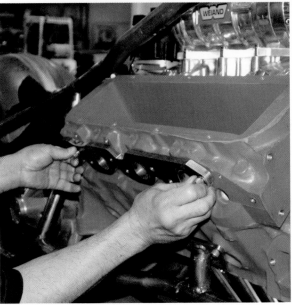
Since the block we were using was made from foam, the parts could only be tack welded in place. The heat of welding would destroy the block.

The most important pipe was the first one as this would set the angle for the rest of the pipes.

You can set the angle of the pipes with a bubble level.

Once I had the angle right, Brian (under the purple hood) tack welded the pipes at the top of the pipe.

By clamping a bar or angle iron to the bottom of the pipe ends, you can guarantee that the alignment will remain perfect.

To make sure that each of the four exhaust pipe ends were in alignment, a length of angle aluminum was clamped to the front and rear tubes, which were tack-welded on the header flange first.

The digital readout on our Mittler Bros. mandrel tubing bender assured us of identical bends on all of the individual exhaust pipes. The only variable to contend with was the slight amount of spring-back when the bender pressure was relieved.

I used a roll bar bender to bend the exhaust pipes and a protractor to match the angles.

We attached the pipes to the base plate with a small tack weld. This held them in proper alignment until we removed each of the headers. Each of the pipes was eventually TIG welded at the mounting plate.

long with a slight bend near the exhaust ports angling the pipes rearward and slightly downward. These eight pipes were then MIG welded to a 1/4-inch steel plate that was machined to match the exhaust gasket to become the header mounting plate. The hardest one was the first pipe as that would determine the angle of the next ones and the angle was chosen by just using common sense. I angled them slightly downward so the exhaust blast would not hit anyone in the face and the bend angle was to keep the width to a minimum (even though the bike is still 56 inches wide as opposed to a stock Boss Hoss or 45-inch width).

Then I held the first pipe in place at the proper rotation and placement as it was tack welded by Brian. It looked great, so it was on to the last pipe on that side (skipping the center two). After that pipe was placed and welded, we cut a piece of angle aluminum and clamped it from the tip of the first pipe to the tip of the last pipe. This allowed us a way to set the center two pipes in place on the same plane as the first and last pipe. It also allowed us the ability to set the distance and clamp the pipes to the angle for proper holding as we welded them in place. After welding, the angle aluminum was removed and the headers were unbolted and taken to the welding table

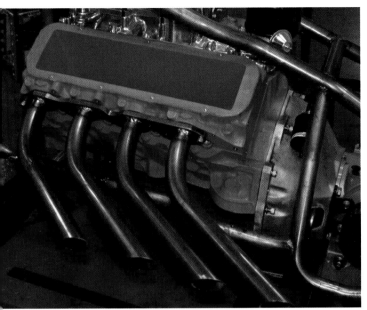

The Zoomies were once again added to check for warpage against to block. As soon as it was determined that the plates were still flat, they were removed and sent to the platers.

The pipes and a few other parts were nickel plated with a smoke color so that they would have an almost "black chrome" look to them. Nickel plating also does not discolor as fast as regular chrome does.

for a 360-degree weld around all the pipe bases. This process was duplicated on the other side as we measured the height of the tip of the exhaust from one side to the other.

The assembly, once finished, was sent to Sheffield Platers in San Diego for a smoked nickel plating.

According to Sheffield, the nickel will not discolor as chrome does when the pipes heat up. With all of the drive train and engine components being readied for Chopper One, it was time to start fabricating a custom tank to wrap around those two Weiand superchargers.

The pipes were added so we could see how they complemented the rest of the bright chrome on the bike. A mix of nickel and chrome provided a bit of variety.

The Drive Train—502 Cubic Inches of Big-Block Chevy!

Chapter Four

Sheet Metal Fabrication—The Custom Tank and Fender

The wheel is my favorite tool. It will make the worst panel look smooth and make you think you know what you are doing. Just roll the metal through it a few times and double-check the shape on the tank or the buck. A little rolling goes a long way to smooth the surface, so don't work it too many times or you will roll it out of alignment.

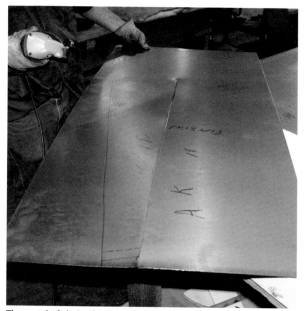

The metal of choice for the tank was AK steel sheet. It is an aluminum kiln-treated steel, which makes it a bit softer to work with.

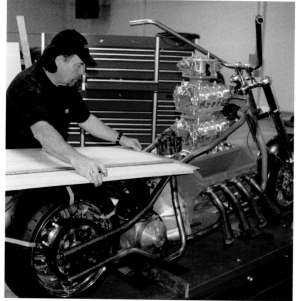

A buck is just a way to get a 3-D view of what you are about to build and a form to check your metal against as you work. I start the buck with the base board, which is little more than a sheet of plywood cut down to a reasonable size to cover the base of the design or the foundation.

How to Build a "Triacontakaipentagon"

Yes, triacontakaipentagon is a word, albeit one that you will most likely never see in print again unless you're into geometry at the college level. A triacontakaipentagon is a 35-sided polygon, which, as you'll see later in this chapter, is what we'll be fabricating for Chopper One's fuel tank! Now, building anything with that many sides and angles is not something that you'll want to do on the fly. Since this is going to be a streamlined custom tank, every panel, angle, joint and edge must be perfectly symmetrical. Plus, the overall shape of the tank must have a defined chopper look. So the obvious question is: How do you make a perfectly symmetrical custom fuel tank with 35 sides? The answer: *patterns!*

Design and pattern making

I cannot imagine building something like a custom motorcycle tank or even a simple fender without having some experience in pattern making or the ability to perform woodwork. Much of what we do in the shop involves drawing, cutting and taping of paper patterns before we cut a single piece of metal. In some cases, we will build a "buck" from wood, or a complete part from solid wood to be used later for forming a 3-D shape of the part. This is called a "hammerform." A hammerform is also a kind of pattern that allows you to place a sheet of metal onto it and, using a hammer, shape it into the form of the wood. Then the wood is removed and the metal can be finish-shaped and fitted into place. Wood is relatively inexpensive when compared to the price of metal. It is also easier to work with, which makes wood pattern making a very cost-effective way to give yourself a spatial view of the metal piece to come.

The base board is then rough trimmed to shape and then "grided-out," making lines 1 inch apart so that the board can be measured and kept symmetrical without having to use a tape measure each time you want to check something. You can simply count the squares; this is particularly handy when working with curves—it gives you a quick visual reference at a glance.

A good pattern can be made of cardboard, paper or, my favorite, thin polycarbonate plastic. My dad was a fabricator and I occasionally saw him use real thin sheet aluminum for his patterns so he could go as far as shaping them once the basic outline was transferred to the proper gauge metal sheet. For simple patterns, I often use paper or thin cardboard, but for complex shapes or ones that require a mounting flange, the clear polycarbonate has a lot of advantages in that you can see through it for transferring mounting points onto the pattern.

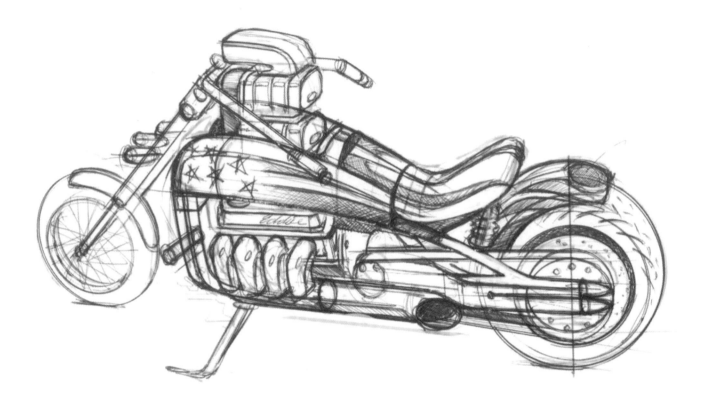

Being a designer and builder, I seldom follow anyone's exact instructions when it comes to the construction of one of my projects. As you can see in a comparison between the finished Chopper One and the original drawings of my old friend Jeff Teague, this build was no exception.

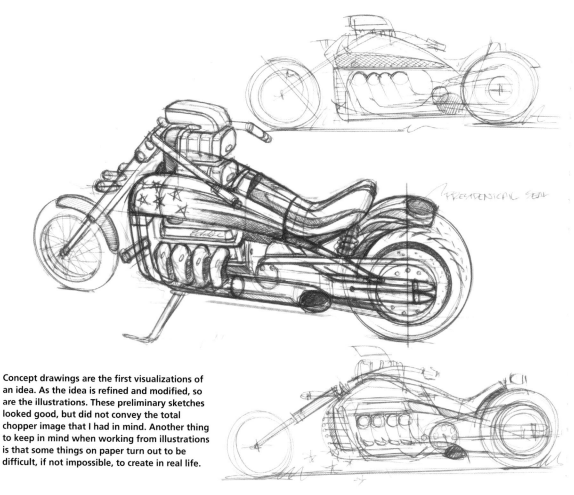

Concept drawings are the first visualizations of an idea. As the idea is refined and modified, so are the illustrations. These preliminary sketches looked good, but did not convey the total chopper image that I had in mind. Another thing to keep in mind when working from illustrations is that some things on paper turn out to be difficult, if not impossible, to create in real life.

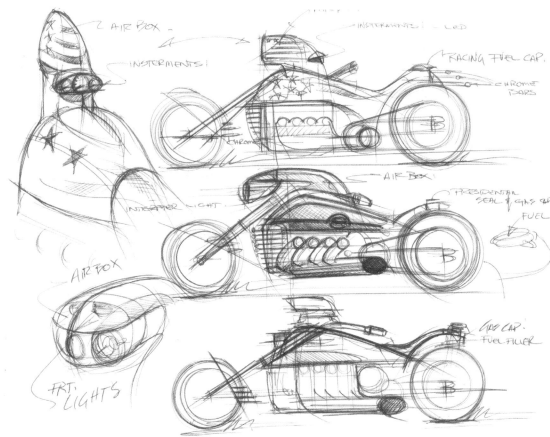

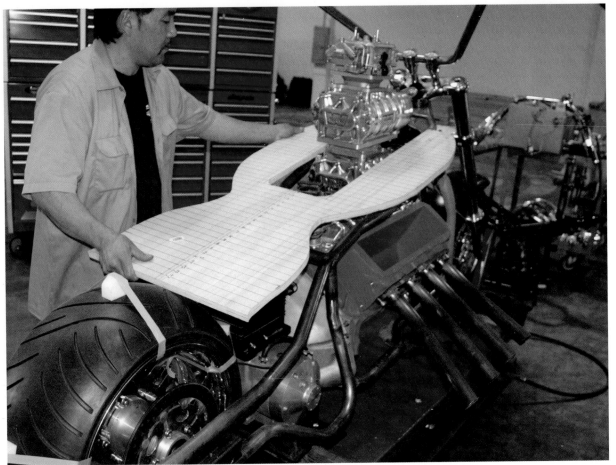

Brian makes a fast check to see if the board clears the double superchargers. It does, and we are off to a good start.

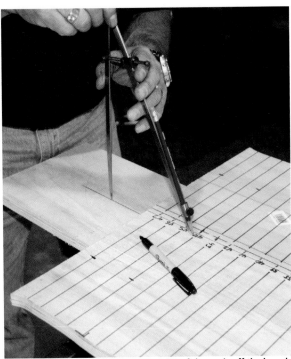

To strike a large arc when the pivot point of the arc is off the board, screw an extra piece of wood on the bottom of the board and use it as a temporary pivot point.

This arc can then be cut out to be the mating line between the board and the rear fender.

It was starting to look as if the scoop (not shown) would be a problem, but I decided to deal with that later.

This view shows the fitting of the baseboard to the frame, as well as a temporary spacer block we taped to the rear tire to hold the rear fender at the proper spacing as it is set on the rear tire. The spacer block height was determined by taking the inside diameter of the fender, subtracting it from the outside diameter of the rear tire, then dividing the result in half. This measurement is now the height of the spacer blocks that will hold the fender exactly the right height off the rear tire, so that they are both concentric. Wheeew! Got that?

We have names for the parts of the buck so we can identify everything—i.e. spine, base plate, ribs, etc.

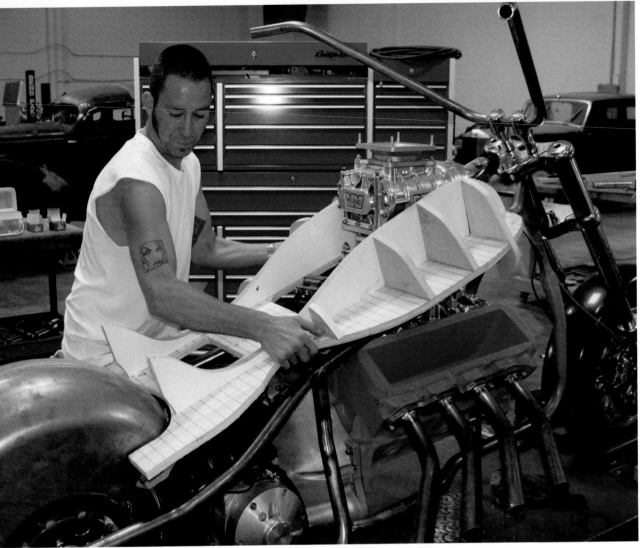

As always, there was constant fitting, testing and marking, and trimming to make it fit better.

If you don't already have a band saw, there is Christmas or your birthday coming up, right?

You can make patterns out of anything you want and you may even find a method or material that no one ever thought of. But remember to stay open to other options and don't be afraid to mix and match your media. I sometimes use a combination of wood or cardboard with clear plastic for my patterns so I can have a "window" to see under the cardboard. Other pattern materials, such as wire, clay, plaster, and screen mesh can all be used with good results; just keep in mind that whatever material you use for a pattern, it should conform to compound bends and curves. If you use a screen material, it can be pressed into a three-dimensional shape such as a compound curve much the same way that the metal can with little effort.

One point to keep in mind concerning templates, whether it is wood, cardboard or plastic, is the thickness of the template material. The thinner the pattern material, the closer to the dimension of the sheet metal and the more accurate the final pattern will be. So foam core is much easier to work with, but when bent, it will have two dimensions—the inside and the outside. The thinner the pattern material is, the closer to the true shape the finished

As soon as the top of the buck was finished, the buck is flipped over and the bottom started so that we will have the tank overhang shape in place.

I used super glue to fasten the small ribs in place before screwing them down, but don't rely on the super glue alone, as it will not take the pounding you may need to do to fit the aluminum to the buck.

Controls and Wiring—How to Make it all Work

Pattern materials

➤ **Paper** is cheap and readily available, but not that strong. Recommended for flat one-time-use patterns only.

➤ **Cardboard** is cheap and stronger than paper, and conforms fairly well to simple contours. Corrugated cardboard, because of the inner layer of corrugation, does not cut cleanly and has a tendency to develop unwanted folds when contours are involved.

➤ **Foam core** is more expensive than paper and cardboard, but very easy to work with. It is lightweight and stronger than cardboard and, like plastic, resists moisture. Foam core is a good choice if you plan to reuse your patterns.

➤ Sheets of thin, **transparent plastic** such as PETG (glycol-modified polyethylene terephthalate) fall into the all-purpose category for pattern making. Vivak is a trade name for PETG plastic and the one that we use quite often at Customs By Eddie Paul. For more information on Vivak or other plastics, talk to the people at Sheffield Plastics in Sheffield, MA.

➤ **Wood** is the pattern material to use for larger three-dimensional objects. A pattern made from wood is referred to as a hammerform if it will be used to shape metal by hammering it to form. Or, in the process of vacuum-forming, the wood pattern is called a plug. A wooden buck is also a type of pattern that serves as a three-dimensional guide for sheet metal work. The type of wood to use for patterns depends largely on the type of pattern that you are making. Common pine is inexpensive and easy to find, but it has a high moisture content, rough grain and texture and has knots. Particle board, or MDF (medium density fiberboard), can make good patterns, but because it only comes in sheet form, it may have to be laminated together to achieve a desired thickness. The pattern wood that I like to use is called Jelutong. It's a fairly expensive hard wood with cutting and shaping qualities of soft wood. Jelutong is not easy to find and is used primarily by professionals as a pattern wood.

➤ Although not a common practice, patterns can be made from thin (26-gauge or so) **sheet metal**. Perhaps the only advantage to patterning with sheet metal is that you'll gain a true sense of the contour that you are making before it's made. It's probably a benefit that only a seasoned fabricator can appreciate.

➤ I first saw **wire mesh** or screen material used by the late Ed "Big Daddy" Roth. Most people think of Roth as a pinstriper—which he was—but he was also one of the all-time great customizers and fabricators. He was in the process of building a custom trike when I caught him making a pattern for the body out of screen. It's easy to cut, conforms to contours, and can be laid flat again to transfer the pattern to metal.

part will be. As a rule, try to match the thickness of pattern material to the actual metal thickness of the part that you're making.

The main tools that I use for pattern making are drawing pens, pencils, rulers and straightedges. A set of "French curves" are also used frequently to transfer a particular shape more accurately onto metal or paper. A set of protractors and a tape measure are essential for designing and making patterns.

The tool required for cutting patterns depends upon the material that is being used. A pair of scissors will cut paper and most cardboard, but some cuts might require a little more precision with a single-edge razor blade or an X-acto knife. I keep a large cutting mat on a wood-top bench to make my cuts on.

Once a pattern is designed, cut and trimmed to the exact shape of the part that is being made, the next step is to transfer the pattern outline to the metal. This can be as simple a process as tracing around the pattern with a felt tip marker. You can also transfer a pattern to metal with a carbide-tipped scribe, or you can spray around the outline of the pattern with a light coat of spray paint as you would with a stencil. Stenciling works well with intricate patterns, but for all-around simplicity and neatness, just marking around the pattern with a fine-point marker works best.

Building A Custom Fuel Tank Or, If At First You Don't Succeed...

As you can see by the accompanying concept illustrations of Chopper One, my original plan was to fabricate a rounded teardrop-shaped tank that might have some resemblance to a fat-bob on steroids! And I planned to do it out of aluminum. The presence of the induction system towering above the top rails of the Chopper One frame totally eliminated the possibility of using the stock Boss Hoss fuel tank. In addition, I wanted the tank, seat and rear fender to flow together as one swoopy, streamlined shape. The one and only thing that bothered me about my original tank idea was that, even though it would be a one-off custom creation, it still would bear some semblance to the run-of-the-mill custom chopper. In spite of this, I went ahead with building the tank as you see in the drawings but, somehow, situations like this have a way of working themselves out in the most, shall I say, *explosive* way!

Gas tanks serve one practical purpose and that is to hold gas. The tank is not a structural part of a motorcycle so, in theory, they can be mounted almost anywhere above the engine. On my last bike project, called "Secret Weapon," the stock fuel tank was totally eliminated in favor of military-style Gerry cans mounted in the saddlebag area. I was able to mount these tanks in the aft position because, being based on a Boss Hoss bike, the Secret Weapon has a strong Holley electric fuel pump.

When I was still kicking around some design possibilities for Chopper One, I considered incorporating the rear fender as part of the tank to increase the fuel-holding capacity.

As you add small pieces of wood you have a solid base to attach the small parts to. Just put them in place and then mark, trim and attach them by gluing and screwing.

After trimming the piece, I tapped it into place with a rubber hammer and then waited a minute for the glue to set so I could attach the screws.

I constantly check the drawings to see if I am on track, even though I may at any point throw the drawing away and shoot off in an entirely new direction.

But I am a traditionalist at heart and the tank belongs above the engine so, for Chopper One, I planned a special tank to wrap around the bottom supercharger and extend into the seat area. Of course, I would have to build it from scratch, as there is nothing off the shelf that will even come close to holding the amount of gas I needed to quench the thirst of this beast.

Although my shop has full capability to fabricate with thermoplastics, I chose to keep it simple and limit my material options to metal for the tank. And since I can weld steel better than I can weld aluminum, I opted for an aluminum tank. This screwed-up logic that I often use probably needs a little explanation. I chose aluminum because it offers an opportunity for me to brush up on one of my skills. I may have over 30 years of fabricating experience, but welding aluminum is one thing that I don't practice regularly since I now have a fulltime welder working for me. And even though I consider it to be more difficult to weld, I find it much easier than steel to shape. So, with time becoming a factor here, the extra hours that it would take me to get my skill level up on welding

aluminum was still less than the total time difference between working with the two different metals. Besides, I've never been known to take the easy road.

For me, the shaping of aluminum was the easy part of making the Chopper One tank, especially since my shop has all the equipment for every step of the fabrication. The tank started out with a wooden "buck." A buck, as I discussed earlier, is a type of pattern, however, it will not actually take the full shape and form of the fuel tank. It will appear more like a bare framework around which I can begin to skin the structure with metal. Once I have a buck in place, I can then visualize what the finished tank will look like, what changes, if any, I need to make, and accurately estimate how much metal will be required. Fabricating with a buck is extremely efficient for a number of reasons. Its main purpose is to keep the tank symmetrical as you pattern the sheet metal. Symmetry is guaranteed if you create your patterns for the left side of a buck and then use those same patterns for the right side. Once the project is complete, you can save the buck to make a duplicate part in the future. I have a fairly large area in my shop dedicated

Once the buck is glued and screwed together, it is time to take it outside to grind the edges so that they all match up and we have a smooth transition from one surface to the next.

Next, we start some practice welds on some strips of the same aluminum I will be building the tank out of. This just gives us a chance to set up the welding rod, gas mixture and welding setting for the tank without having to ruin the tank in the process.

to the storage of bucks from past projects such as body parts from the cars of *The Fast and The Furious* and *2Fast 2Furious.*

The first part of the buck construction requires that you lay down a center spine that will give you the profile of the shape you want for the final tank. The lower part of this section will have to be cut and fitted to the bike, so it may require a set of center spines on each side of the superchargers instead of one down the center. This part of the buck is the most critical and should be measured and cut with precision and patience; rushing through the basic framework could have detrimental effects on alignment, symmetry and overall appearance.

Once the main section of the buck is made, it can be attached to the frame at any point of contact. The buck is attached only temporarily, so you must use existing mounts on the frame or, most likely, clamps to hold it securely in place. When the exact position of the buck is determined, clearly mark the location so that you can remove and replace the buck as you add stations to it. The main section of the buck is called the "spine," which runs the length of the part that you're making—in this case, the fuel tank. The sections that comprise the width of the part are called "stations." There can be as many stations as you want or need; the more stations you add to the spine the more accurate the buck will be. Stations add the detail to a buck so the bigger the buck, or the more contours the buck has, the more stations there should be.

The best material for this type of buck is plywood with a thickness of 1/2 to 3/4 inch. Some fabricators choose particleboard, which can also work well, depending on the method of assembly. If the buck components are glued together, then particleboard is a viable option. However, if wood screws are used (and this is my preference), then plywood is the better choice as it has fewer tendencies to

crack. Another benefit of using screws is that the individual pieces of the buck can be taken apart and modified or adjusted.

After the main spine or spines are in place, the stations are then cut and attached starting from the front. With a piece of cardboard pressed up flat against the spine for a template, I make one side of the first station, marking the shape and trimming and fitting until I am happy with the shape. I make sure to hold it against the spine at the same height so it can be returned to the same spot between trimmings. Once I am content with the shape, I transfer the shape to a piece of plywood, allowing for the spine thickness and notching the center part to fit over the spine, which I will also have to cut to accept the first station.

At this point I sometimes go ahead and notch the entire spine every few inches so it will accept each station as they are fabricated. This notch will be the width of the plywood (or particleboard) and half the depth of the spine at that point (i.e.: if the spine is 6 inches deep at station four, then the cut will be 3 inches deep at that station location). A small 1-inch-by-1-inch 90-degree shelf bracket (available at any hardware store) can be added at each station to anchor it to the station. Once the spine and stations of the buck are finished and assembled, the next step is to sand or file the profile of each station so that the edges form an even smooth contour.

The buck should not be confused with a hammerform. The buck that I made for the Chopper One fuel tank will be used for checking the fit of the metal as each piece is fabricated. A wooden hammerform is used as a three-dimensional backing for sheet metal as you hammer directly onto it.

With a complete wooden buck shaped to my tank design, I began the actual fabrication of the inner section of the tank with 1/8-inch 3003 H14 aluminum plate. I made the

Sheet Metal Fabrication—The Custom Tank and Fender

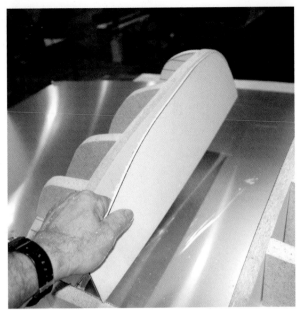

The plug is taken to a sheet of half-hard 3000 series aluminum and the base pattern is traced out of the aluminum and then cut. This will be the base plate for the tank. It will be soft and floppy until the vertical parts are added, but the shape will give it the strength as we add metal and shape or form it.

The inner plates are added by first trimming them 1/4 larger than the pattern (notice the round disc we added to the felt tip marker for a tracer). This is a simple way to add a flange to a curve.

We use Bosch electric sheers or a saber saw for rough cutting aluminum. Be sure to lube your blade to avoid binding. A spray of WD-40 every once in a while makes a world of difference.

Most of the bucks are made from wood or particle board and are strong enough to hold the aluminum flat between them as you tap the edges over the shape. You can save the forms for future jobs if you think you will be making something like it again.

inner section first because it forms the foundation of my design around which the rest of the tank will be shaped. Each sheet of the 3000 alloy was annealed with the rosebud-tipped Esab gas torch to facilitate workability. For those of you who would like to learn more about aluminum alloys and general metallurgy, I devoted a complete chapter on the subject in my *Custom Bodywork Handbook*. Once the inner tank and understructure were made and tack-welded together, the mounting brackets and the fittings for the petcock and fuel gauge sending unit were welded on.

The outer walls of the tank were made next. For this I also used 3003 H14 aluminum alloy, but with a thickness of only .050, or 16 gauge. The forming qualities of the 3000-series aluminum of this thickness did not require annealing for me to attain the outer tank shape. I patterned and cut the pieces for the left side of the tank and then duplicated each piece for the right side. Each piece was carefully roughed in with a plastic ball mallet on a sandbag, wheeled into smooth form on the Eastwood English wheel, and then fitted to the buck. You can refer to the accompanying photos in this chapter for a look at how I performed the various processes.

By clamping the wood to each side of the metal the metal will have enough support to keep it flat as you slowly tap the edges over the "hammer form." You will need to move the clamps as you work.

The wood makes an inexpensive form to use for shaping edges. These edges will add a lot of strength to the otherwise flat metal.

The finished metal has a nice flange running around the perimeter that is hard to make any other way. It all only took a few hours and about $10 worth of material.

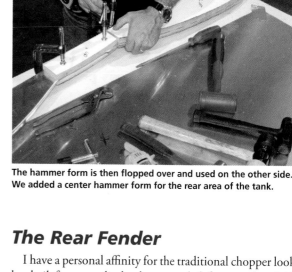

The hammer form is then flopped over and used on the other side. We added a center hammer form for the rear area of the tank.

I don't often recommend a direct competitor's product but, in this case, I have to make an exception. Metal fabricator Ron Covell is a name that many of you might be familiar with. Ron has a series of videos and DVDs on many of the topics that my books and DVD/videos cover. Ron's video on motorcycle tank fabrication has some excellent information for anybody who plans to build a custom tank. Ron's videos are available through The Eastwood Co. along with the Eddie Paul line of videos and fabrication tools that are sold under the Eastwood label.

The Rear Fender

I have a personal affinity for the traditional chopper look: hardtail frame, radical rake, extended front end, suicide shift and "ape-hangers." My last ride, a '70 Shovelhead, was a perfect example of this. It didn't have any of the custom fender treatments that are so prevalent on today's custom bikes. In fact, it had no fender up front, and a short bobbed trailer fender over the rear tire. This is the area where Chopper One will tend to stray away from the traditional chopper look that I like. I decided to go fender-less up front, but somehow streamline the design of the

The second side is shaped with the same hammer form as the first side and the part is ready to be unclamped and welded to the tank base plate.

Within a few hours we have a section that can be added to the center well of the gas tank and a good support for the rest of the tank.

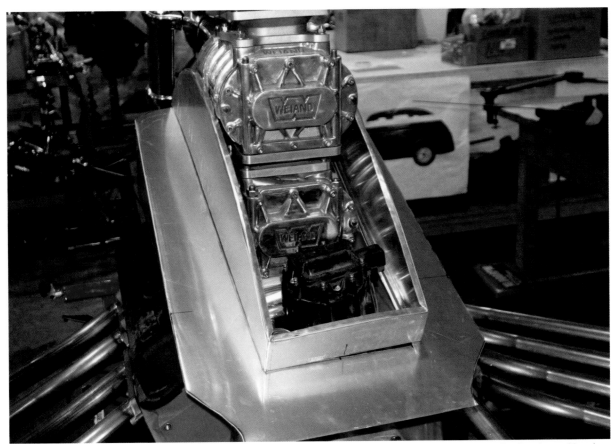

Notice the top flanges are facing inward. This was simply changed by bending the rear bends 180 degrees the opposite direction making the flanges face outward.

rear fender and incorporate it into the design of the fuel tank. My reason for this is a simple one: I wanted to have a larger "canvas" on which to display the red-white-and-blue paint scheme that I had in mind.

Aside from style considerations, a fender is a fairly easy component to design and fabricate. As with the tank, the rear fender would be the first of two that I made for Chopper One. The first version that I made was actually a modification to a stamped steel blank that came from Victor at California Boss Hoss. The blank was an ultra-wide

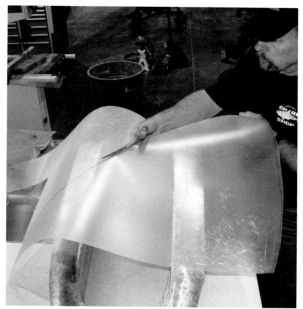

After setting the new piece on the bike, I decided to make another piece with a curved rear section, instead of a square section.

The center section and top plate were added and welded in place as the tank started to really take shape. The Vivak is a thin plastic we use for patterns.

piece designed to be used with the new 300mm Avon rear tire and custom billet wheel that also came from Victor.

With the Chopper One frame and first tank mocked up and secured to our Ranger RML-750HD motorcycle lift, I was able to slide the rear wheel and tire assembly into place and prop the black fender up to get an idea of what I needed to do to it. I built the Chopper One frame especially to accommodate the Avon 300mm tire and wheel combo and I was now beginning to visualize what an awesome and extreme bike this would be!

As impressive as it looked, the fender still needed some trimming to fit. It also needed a touch of something to tie it into the rest of the bike. (To a customizer, everything needs something!) It was here that I began to deviate from the concept illustration of Chopper One. Rather than incorporate the rear fender into the tank, I decided to tie it into the frame instead. I would trim the blank and then add a couple of wing-like elements to resemble the rear frame tubes. I would scale the tube size down to a 1-inch diameter and bend the "wings" to the contour of the fender with the ends extending off the fender at the same angle as the frame tubes. A picture is worth more than all those words so you can look at the accompanying photos to get a better idea what I was working toward.

This was not a radical modification to the rear fender, but it would still set it apart from all the others I have seen. Bending the tubes was simply a matter of matching the radius of the rear fender. To accomplish this, I measured the outside diameter of the fender at 29.75 inches, and then proceeded to bend a section of tubing on my Eagle tube-bending machine to the same diameter. I left the last 6 inches of the tube straight so it would level off somewhat like a tail fin. The last modification made to the fender blank was the addition of a rectangular license plate housing.

While Brian and I were finishing up on the fender and

mounts for the frame, the tank was being finish-welded by our full-time (at that time) welder who, for the sake of this story, we'll call Dick. Although everything was coming together smoothly, I just wasn't quite satisfied with the overall look of the tank and rear fender. Not only did it not match my original concept, but the two components just didn't seem to have the particular silhouette that I was trying to achieve. So what happened next actually turned out to be a blessing in disguise.

The Tank that Rocked the House!

Brian and I had just stepped out into the shop when, all of a sudden, a loud explosion rattled the windows and shook the rafters of my 25,000-square-foot shop! We immediately turned to the source of the blast and our eyes went straight to the welding bench, on top of which sat a torn shell of what looked like the new aluminum Chopper One fuel tank. It looked like a grenade had exploded inside of it! We walked over to the bench where Dick was still standing, in shock, and fortunately unhurt, over the tank remains. As it turned out, Dick, after welding the tank up, took it upon himself to "*pressure test*" the structure by direct application of about 80psi from the shop's main air system. I thought to myself, "*80psi?!* What was this idiot trying to accomplish? And at what pressure was he planning to stop filling my new tank with air?" Where he got the idea to do this is still a mystery, but because of this and other reasons, Dick is no longer under my employ.

My thought now is that if an average guy like Dick, an adequate welder but otherwise not very skilled, can make a blundering mistake by confusing the process of a "pressure test" with a "leak test," I think it's a procedure that warrants a brief discussion here.

Sheet Metal Fabrication—The Custom Tank and Fender

Each piece had to be made as an exact mirror image of the other so that we wound up with a symmetrical design.

With a hammer in one hand and a MIG torch in the other hand, Brian takes it one weld at a time—weld, tap into alignment, then weld again.

The top rear fender panel is next for fabrication.

After performing a fabrication of or modification to a motorcycle fuel tank, the structure must be made absolutely leak-proof before the first drop of gas goes in. The only way to insure that a tank is leak-proof is to perform a simple test. Perhaps Dick's problem was that he associated the tank that he was welding to his welding tanks, which are canisters designed specifically for containing gas at high pressure levels. Well, the gas that goes into a fuel tank is a liquid, and certainly is not under pressure of any kind. Therefore, we want to test a new fuel tank for *leaks* rather than its pressure capacity. Applying excessive air pressure to any structure not so designed is extremely dangerous because air is compressible, and pressurizing a tank with air can create a dangerous situation that can culminate in

an explosion. So don't be a Dick! Test a tank for leaks, *not pressure.*

My self-imposed deadline for the completion of Chopper One was fast approaching. I had made a commitment to my book publisher to have the bike ready for the 2005 Specialty Equipment Market Association show, as well as for the build-up photography for this book. Brian, the manager of my shop and a former editor of *Car Craft*, *Sport Compact Car* and *Drag Racing* magazines, was not only working alongside me building Chopper One, but also helping out with the book too. We were literally building, writing about, and photographing each step of the project all at once, along with handling a multitude of other jobs and tasks as well. The hectic schedule that we were dealing with during the entire Chopper One build included filming the pilot for an upcoming reality show based on the work here at Customs By Eddie Paul, manufacturing tools for companies such as Eastwood and Autobody Tool Mart, designing an explosive for the Department of Defense (top secret!), developing my Cylindrical Energy Module (CEM) 12-cylinder rotary engine, and tooling up my shop for 3-D digitizing and CNC routing capabilities to build the real-life versions of the animated racecars for the upcoming Disney/Pixar movie called *Cars*, just to name a few. As crazy as all of this may sound, it's pretty much the daily routine here, which is why Brian and I have learned to become jacks-of-all-trades over the years.

Having to fabricate a new fuel tank from scratch was not something that made things any easier, but the silver lining in this cloud was that I was going to totally redesign the tank and rear fender with a look that would *really* rock the house (and without the explosion)! The first tank design came out exactly the way it was supposed to, but I just wasn't happy with it. For this reason, the lines of my new tank would follow a more contemporary style and, as per

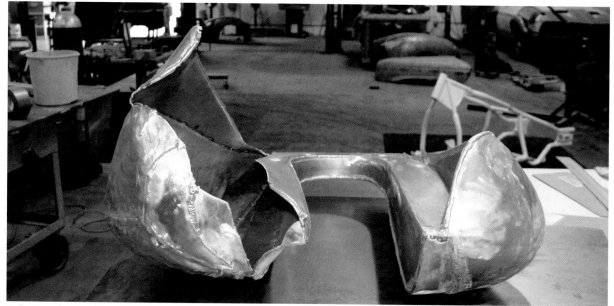

Unfortunately, one of our workers took it upon himself to pressure test the tanks to 80 psi. Predictably, it went boom.

the original concept, incorporate the seat area and rear fender all in one piece.

When I told Brian the new plan, he was not the least bit shocked. He just calmly walked over to the steel rack and dragged out a 4 x 8-foot sheet of 18-gauge steel and laid it out on the table so we could start over.

I started with the inner structure again as I did with tank number one, however, the material this time was 18-gauge steel. Working with sheet steel would save us a little time because no annealing would be required and the entire job could be welded with the faster MIG. I then cut the base plate. This base plate would be the foundation of the tank and would have to support the weight of the fuel, the seat section, rear fender and rider. It would also serve to define the overall shape of the tank, as it did with the first design. It needed to be symmetrical or the whole tank would be wrong. I sometimes design and cut half the tank profile (from front to back) out of plastic and flop the pattern over to make sure it will have the exact same profile on both sides when I transfer the design from plastic to metal.

From this point on it was pretty smooth sailing with our familiar teamwork getting us past the tank crisis without further incident. The new and more elaborate tank took less than two days for us to design and build. This was followed by another day of welding with Brian at the torch this time, and also performing all testing for leaks.

So that's how the world's first and only "triacontakaipentagon" Boss Hoss chopper tank came to be; a 35-sided, perfectly symmetrical, one-piece tank/seat/fender design. Then it was over to the body and paint department for molding, prep and paint.

Working With Sheet Metal

Sheet metal fabrication is nothing less than an art, and the more artistic you are, the more creative you can get with your projects. The creative aspect of sheet metal fabrication

The tank was almost finished before the mishap. This shows the power of air and why you need to know what you are doing before you do it. One or two pounds of air would have been fine, but not 80.

is not something that can easily be demonstrated. Creativity is the product of ideas, and ideas come from all walks of life, including reading books such as this.

When you see a master craftsman at work with a sheet of metal, it's nothing short of amazing how easy they make it look. Unlike engine mechanics, today's fabricators still rely on many of the old world techniques and tools that have been used for decades. When it comes to forming sheet metal, nothing has replaced the basic body hammer for making repairs or for customizing. Of course, you'll need more than just a body hammer to tackle a job such as a motorcycle fuel tank, but compared to an engine mechanic, the tools required for fabricating are relatively few and inexpensive. For example, there are several ways to

Take a Leak...Test

Method one: Here's a simple and safe leak test that I recommend you perform after fabricating a fuel tank. First, seal off all openings (i.e. fuel filler, vents, etc.) with duct tape. Next, install a barbed hose fitting with NPT threads to the threaded petcock valve opening. Attach a hose connected to a regulated air supply to the barbed fitting. Be absolutely sure to have the regulator closed so that no air is flowing when you connect the hose to the tank.

Before you introduce air into the tank, have a few ounces of a soapy water solution and a brush at the ready. Now, very slowly, open the regulator valve just slightly until the gauge begins to indicate no more than 2 or 3 psi (pounds per square inch). If the pressure that you apply becomes excessive, the duct tape over the fuel filler opening should give way and release the pressure. This is not guaranteed so, to be safe, monitor the pressure gauge carefully. With the air in the tank regulated at a steady 2 or 3 psi, liberally brush the tank along the seams with the mixture of soapy water. If you have a leak, you will see bubbles immediately. Mark the precise location where the bubbles are forming and proceed with the remainder of the tank until all welded seams are tested. The accompanying photos of this process show leak testing of the second Chopper One tank for which I had Brian perform the duties.

Another way to test a tank for leaks involves the opposite of pressure: vacuum. One of the special products that I manufacture are deep sea camera housings that must withstand extreme pressures of up to 300 psi at a depth of about 600 feet. Many professional divers, including the Cousteaus, rely on my housings to protect their very expensive photographic equipment from the harsh salt water.

Vacuum-testing for leaks is equally reliable, however, to perform this type of testing, you'll need a vacuum pump (either power or manual) and a sensitive detector to trace the sound of leaking air. You can use a mechanic's stethoscope on the lower end of the budget, or you can get a bit more high-tech with an ultrasonic detector.

Whichever testing device is used, the procedure is fairly simple. Pull a vacuum on the tank and listen for a leak. Vacuum, unlike pressure, is measured in inches of mercury. This test requires no more than 5 to 10 inches of vacuum. Since this is an audible test rather than a visual one with bubbles indicating a leak, you can only attain a close approximation of

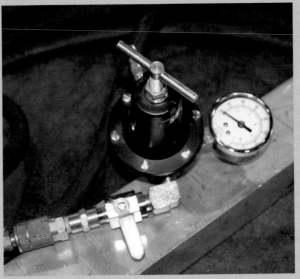

An inline air regulator is used to keep the pressure down to no more than 2 psi as we test the tank for leaks.

Even if a tank passes the leak test, it is best to use gas tank sealer, just in case. The secret to sealing a gas tank is not just the perfect weld, but the use of a chemical "gas tank sealer." It is impervious to gasoline and you can simply pour it in the tank and slush it around (rotating the tank every 5 minutes until the stuff cures up in about one hour). That's it. This product is available from The Eastwood Co.

the leak, but it should be good enough to perform the necessary fix.

Method three: This third leak solution is not a test, but a preventative measure that should be done regardless of how you test your tank for leaks. Every fuel tank that I build, restore, or repair gets treated to a "slushing compound," even if it tests negative

A solution of soap and water can be brushed over the outer surface of the tank. When you see small bubbles, you know you have a leak.

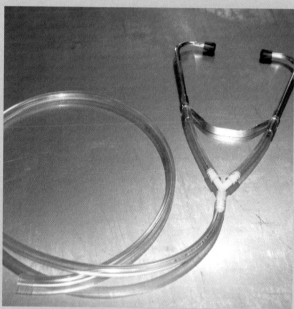

You can also use a stethoscope to listen for air leaks. This works if the shop is not too loud.

for any leaks. Slushing compound is otherwise known as fuel tank sealer. The tank sealer that I used for Chopper One is a product from The Eastwood Company. It's a one-quart one-part liquid that is poured into the tank and "slushed around' until the metal is thoroughly coated. Once cured, the tank is ready to hold fuel.

The tank has to be rotated until the tank sealer sets up. Some projects take 10 minutes, some up to two hours. So, invite a friend over for a tank rotating party.

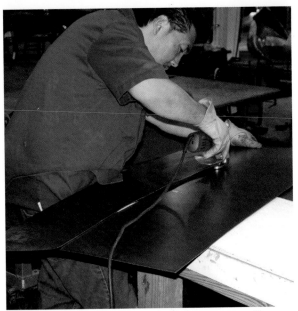

Since the last tank was destroyed I decided to start over with a new design and a new material—steel. It was easier to work with in the time we had left and we have an abundance of it in stock. I was not all that happy with the original design, anyway, so there was a silver lining in the whole ordeal.

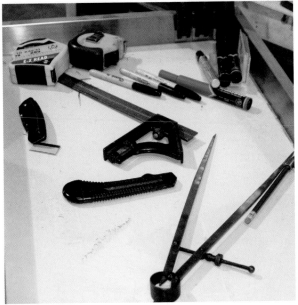

These are some of the basic tools required for performing pattern and layout work.

make a simple bend in a sheet of metal. You can often work a sheet by hand or you can use an object in your garage such as the edge of a workbench to get a fairly straight bend or curve. You can make clean, sharp bends using a hand brake or a shop vise or, for longer bends, you can use a length of angle iron edge as a clamp along the edge of your bench top as a makeshift metal brake. Then when you find yourself bending metal on a more frequent basis, you can invest in a sheet metal brake. From there, it won't be long before you're adding other fabrication equipment, such as shrinkers, stretchers and rollers.

When it comes to the tools for metal fabrication, you can buy special equipment for every process involved, or you can rely on your ingenuity and get by with what you already have out in your garage. One rule that I live by when it comes to tools is: always buy high-quality tools. You can refer to the Manufacturers Source Guide in Chapter 7 for a complete listing of my tool, equipment and material suppliers. Another good source for tool information and fabrication techniques can be found in my previous book called *Eddie Paul's Custom Bodywork Handbook* from Krause Publications.

A Crash Course In Basic Welding

Welding is a craft that all metal fabricators need to be familiar with. There are many forms of welding and different types of welding equipment, most of which do not pertain to the fabrication of Chopper One. Welding machines are in no short supply in my shop. Since the projects that I take on frequently involve critical welding of exotic metal alloys, I need that type of equipment on hand. The machines that see the most frequent use

on a daily basis, however, are my Esab MigMaster 250 and Esab HeliArc 252. We're not exclusive to Esab equipment, however; we also use the Lincoln Power MIG 200, Square Wave TIG 175 Pro, SP135 Plus MIG (a smaller 110v machine), Pro Cut 55 plasma cutter, and Miller water-cooled Synchrowave 250.

The most common type of welder used for motorcycle and automotive customizing is the MIG, or "wire-feed", welder. MIG is an acronym for "metal inert gas." MIG welding is the easiest form of welding to learn. Without any welding experience at all, most people can pick up a MIG gun and, with a little practice, be able to lay down a nice even bead within a few hours. TIG stands for "tungsten inert-gas". TIG welding requires quite a bit more practice. Before jumping into TIG welding, I highly recommend starting off with basic oxygen-acetylene gas welding first, as the techniques involved are very similar.

For home use, I recommend a smaller and more affordable MIG welder that operates on 110-volt house current. Not only do the smaller welders require less power, but they can also be used with flux-core welding wire to eliminate the need for renting a tank of argon/CO_2 gas. With a 110-volt machine such as the Lincoln SP135 Plus, the limit on the thickness of mild steel that you can weld without compromising penetration and strength is a quarter of an inch. Fortunately, this covers just about every type of welding that you might encounter when fabricating a custom chopper.

Perhaps the two main considerations for purchasing a welder for home use (aside from quality) are cost and your source of available power. A 110-volt MIG welder will operate on a standard 20- or 30-amp power circuit, and the cost will run anywhere between $300 to $800. If your garage is outfitted with a 50- or 60-amp 220-

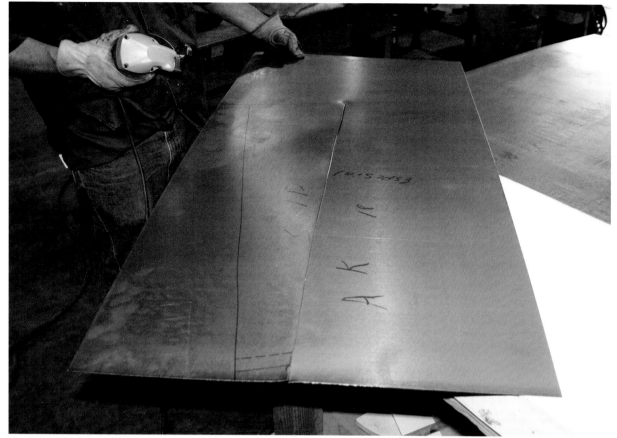

The dash had to be as unique as the rest of the bike and my intention was for the dash to fill in the tank well so you could not see the bottom supercharger, You can't buy an "off the shelf" dash for this application, so it was over to our wood shop to fab up a custom plastic dash.

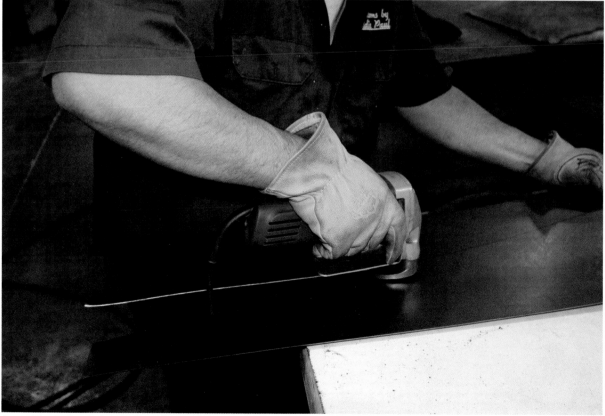

A set of Bosch electric shears will cut the metal like it was paper.

The base plate is laid down and the vertical supercharger surround is cut and checked for fit, much as we did in the aluminum tank. However, steel is much stronger and will not require a flange for support.

The base plate is bent on the marks, not only for design, but for strength as well. Slight bends will add a lot of strength to a flat piece of metal. If done well, they can also be very attractive.

With the well tack welded in place, the bottom is patterned and the tank is under way. The ETC (Estimated Time of Completion) is two days. We definitely saved time by using steel instead of aluminum.

The gas cap is next to be started and a trial fit on top of one of the gas tank panels is in order to see if any further modifications are required.

A miscalculation in measuring the battery location resulted in a fast cut and a quick modification to allow for the required clearance.

A few more panels and the tank was starting to take shape.

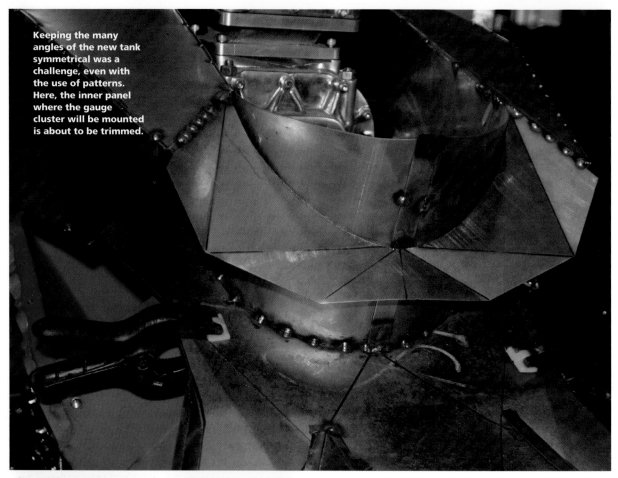

Keeping the many angles of the new tank symmetrical was a challenge, even with the use of patterns. Here, the inner panel where the gauge cluster will be mounted is about to be trimmed.

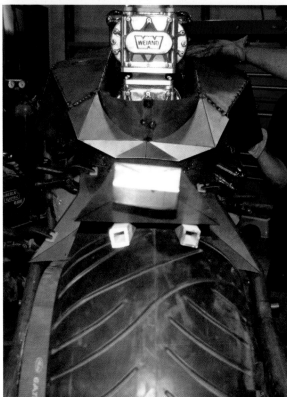

From the rear you can see the rear fender and tank as it starts to take shape. We use a set of square aluminum tubes for rear fender spacers as we fab up the assembly. You can see the way we tack weld the panel in place as we proceed.

volt single-phase power circuit and your bank account can handle it, you can open up your options to include a full-size MIG welder that will give you the capability of tackling much heavier metals up to a half-inch in thickness. A full-size MIG will start at about $1,000 or so and go up from there.

A fully equipped metal fabricator must have a good MIG machine as well as a TIG welder, an oxygen/acetylene gas welding setup, and a plasma cutter. A regular arc welder, often referred to as a stick welder or "buzz box", can be used in some instances but really should be left for heavy construction and welding that does not require neatness and precision. TIG welding is the most precise form of welding, but also requires the most practice to become proficient at. On the other hand, a MIG welder is an extremely versatile machine and some can even convert to TIG if so equipped.

If you plan to outfit your shop or home garage with welding equipment, my suggestion is to research your choices based on the type of welding that you plan to do. You can refer to my *Custom Bodywork Handbook* for a more in-depth discussion on metal and welding, or you can check with welding equipment manufacturers such as Esab for even more technical information on the subject. I've outlined some of the advantages and disadvantages that I've observed with different types of welders to hopefully help get you headed in the right direction.

Every inch of the tank is ground down in preparation for the filler. We use coarse grit (16-grit) so the filler will "bite" into the surface of the metal and mechanically bond to it.

Oxygen-acetylene Gas Welders

Oxygen-acetylene, or simply "gas" welding, is the basic form of welding that has been around for well over half a century. There is no electrical arc involved and there are many processes that can be performed with a gas welding kit that has a full assortment of torch tips. The main disadvantage to gas welding at an entry level is excessive heat that tends to warp sheet metal, but as your skill level rises, the tendency to warp metal lessens. In my shop, I use the Esab Oxweld Trade Master welding and cutting kit (number 18835). This complete kit includes regulators for both oxygen and acetylene gases, a torch handle and hose, plus a variety of welding tip sizes, a cutting tip, and a "rosebud" tip for heating. Although we seldom weld with the oxy-acetylene welder, the cutting tip works well for rough cutting, and the rosebud tip is what we use to anneal metal.

Oxygen-acetylene welding advantages:

1 Portability—A small kit with small tanks is completely self-contained. Requires no outside power source.

2 Versatility—A complete set of tips will allow you to weld, cut, heat and solder most metals.

3 Affordability—Cost for a basic starter kit is fairly low at $100-$300, depending on if it's new or used equipment.

Oxygen-acetylene welding disadvantages:

1 Tanks must be rented or purchased. The need to refill often occurs at the most inconvenient time. Also, acetylene gas is extremely explosive.

2 Generates more heat than arc-type welding and tends to warp thin metals.

3 Difficult to use. However, once you become accomplished at gas welding, skill with all other types of welding is easily acquired.

There are almost too many choices when it comes to welders and brands. We have an assortment of the best and found that a cheap welder is a bad investment. Buy the best you can afford and it should last you a lifetime. This Miller water-cooled TIG welder has been in my shop for many years without a problem.

MIG/TIG Welders

MIG welding is a type of arc welding with convenient one-handed operation using a gun to feed the wire (which also strikes the arc) to the metal. When the gun is triggered, the wire starts to feed and a shielding gas is automatically emitted at the nozzle to prevent the metal from oxidizing. Different types of shielding gas are required for different metals, however, for mild steel welding, a mixture of 75-percent argon/25-percent carbon-dioxide works best. Some 110-volt MIGs allow the use of a special welding wire known as "flux core." Upon striking the arc, flux core wire releases its own shielding gas, thus eliminating the need for supplied gas from a tank. MIG welders come in different amperages. The higher the amperage rating, the thicker the metal you can weld.

Unlike oxygen-acetylene gas welding, which always uses the same two gases, MIG and TIG welding can use a different type and/or a mixture of gases, depending on the type of metal being welded. Because of this, I have several welders in my shop, each one dedicated for use with specific metals. The three most common metals that we fabricate with are mild steel, aluminum and stainless steel. Keep in mind that certain types of metal can only be welded with certain types of welders and some metals can't be welded at all. But for most mild steel jobs, a mixture of 75-percent argon/25-percent carbon-dioxide (a standard mix available from any welding gas supplier) is used. For most aluminum welding, 100 percent argon is used. And for stainless steel, the argon is mixed with 2 percent oxygen. Of course, there are other combinations of gases that are used for other applications, and not all fabricators may agree with my recommendations, but these are the gases that work best in my shop. It should be noted that for those of you who might not want to keep so many different tanks of gas on hand, 100 percent argon can be used for most mild steel, aluminum and stainless welding.

TIG, or HeliArc (HeliArc is a registered trade name of the Esab company), welding also uses an electrical arc, however, unlike MIG welding, a TIG welder does not feed the wire through a gun. A TIG welder uses a torch handle with a tungsten tip through which the arc is struck. The tungsten tip is enclosed by a cup, which directs the

If you are planning to do a lot of MIG welding, this can of anti-splatter will be your best friend. This material keeps the weld splatter from sticking to the rest of the parts (except glass) you are welding.

There are a lot of accessories that come with the welders. This little TIG tip holder is one of the better ones as it keeps all your tips handy and organized.

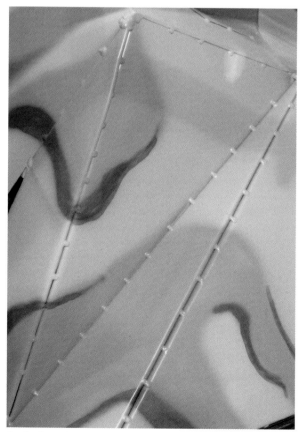

On the Secret Weapon, I used a series of intermittent welds, not only for temporary holding, but for the finish weld as well. They are strong and they look good.

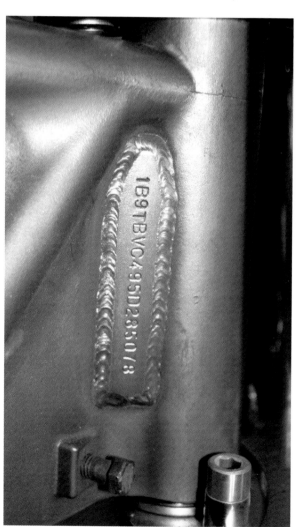

The bike's ID is TIG welded onto the side of the cast-iron neck so the bike can later be identified during the registration process. In a case like this, if the weld looks good you will not need to grind it down.

Sheet Metal Fabrication—The Custom Tank and Fender

ESAB makes one of the best welding systems around. We have the MIG, TIG and a few plasma cutters. ESAB also makes a good 110 plasma cutter with a built-in compressor so you will not need to hook up to an air supply as you cut.

shielding gas around the weld area. TIG welding is a two-handed process with one hand holding the torch handle and the other feeding the welding rod.

To achieve the proper heat penetration for a strong weld with either MIG or TIG, control settings for amperage, gas flow, wire feed speed (MIG only), and polarity (TIG only) are important adjustments that change with various types of metals and thicknesses.

Eye protection is an absolute must-use piece of equipment for all types of welding, but particularly when an electrical arc is involved. You should refer to the manufacturer of your welder for recommendation of the proper level of shading required to protect your eyesight.

MIG welding advantages:

1 A 110-volt gasless MIG (fitted with flux-core wire rather than a tank of gas) is the most portable type of welder, providing you have access to 110-volt power.
2 A shop-sized MIG can handle metal thicknesses up to a half-inch.

3 Consumables (wire, replacement tips, etc.) are very inexpensive.
4 Very easy to learn and use, most people learn to produce a respectable weld the first day.
5 Some MIGs are convertible, allowing you to change setups for TIG and plasma cutting.

MIG welding disadvantages:

1 Must have electricity to operate; shop-sized machines must have a 220-volt single- or three-phase power outlet.
2 Although smaller 110-volts MIGs cost less than $500, the larger machines can run well over $1,000.

TIG welding advantages:

1 TIG welding is capable of producing the neatest and often strongest welds.
2 Certain metals can only be welded with TIG.
3 A TIG welder can be controlled to generate the least

The latest tool acquisition at **Customs By Eddie Paul** is this PlasmaCAM DHC, which takes plasma cutting to a whole new level of precision and repeatability. The DHC is a two-axis CNC (computer numberic control) machine that can be programmed to cut anything from simple brackets and gussets to intricate designs. Our machine uses the Hypertherm Powermax 1250 plasma cutter.

amount of heat during welding

4 There are no sparks or weld spatter.

5 No wire spool to change for welding different types/ thicknesses of metal.

TIG welding disadvantages:

1 Requires much practice to become proficient at TIG welding.

2 Tanks of different gases required for certain metals.

3 Two-hand operation is sometimes cumbersome.

4 Although TIG welding produces beautiful welds, the process is much more time-consuming than MIG.

Plasma Cutting

The plasma cutter may sound like a space-age device, but it's actually quite a simple one. All matter on Earth takes on one of four forms: solid, liquid, gas, or plasma. And all is related to temperature. When a solid is heated to its melting point, a liquid is formed. Heating the liquid to its point of evaporation turns it into gas. And heating gas to an extremely high temperature produces *plasma*. Most of the matter in our universe (the sun, for example) is plasma matter. But due to its extremely high temperature, the only plasma that you'll likely find on Earth is in lightning or coming out of a plasma cutter nozzle!

So a plasma cutter is basically a machine that creates and harnesses the energy of a plasma arc. Without getting into a boring lesson on the physics and science of plasma, suffice

it to say that using a plasma cutter is the fastest and cleanest way to make flame cuts in metal without the residual heat generated by a conventional torch.

Because of the great amount of metal work that we do, my shop has several plasma cutters on hand ranging from small 110-volt models such as the Esab Handy Plasmarc 125, to the heavy-duty 220-volt Powercut 650 that can slice through a 3/4-inch slab of steel like it was butter. Another good quality plasma cutter is the Pro Cut 55 made by Lincoln Electric. Like welders, plasma cutters range in size and cost from small to large.

Hypertherm is another company that manufactures high-quality plasma cutters. We use the Powermax 600 for light cutting, the G3 Series Powermax 1000 for heavy-duty requirements, and our CNC plasma cutter is outfitted with the Hypertherm Powermax 1250, which is capable of slicing through steel up to 3/4 inch thick.

Using a plasma cutter is not only easy, but it's a lot of fun! Because of the accuracy of the plasma arc and the thick metal-cutting capability, I was able to design some very intricate brackets of 1/4-inch thick steel for Chopper One and cut them out in a matter of minutes. Cutting the pieces for Chopper One's unique "triacontakaipentagon" fuel tank/rear fender was a different story.

Sheet Metal Fabrication—The Custom Tank and Fender

Chapter Five

Controls and Wiring—
How to Make it all Work

One of the handiest tools that you can use when bending tubing is this little digital level. It will provide the angle in tenths of a degree, giving you the ability to make multiple bends in any direction and keep the symmetry of angles.

The factors that are most important in enhancing or inhibiting the rider's control of a motorcycle are much the same as those of a driver in a car. How a driver sits in relation to the steering wheel, shifter and pedals is essential to good performance driving. For the rider of a motorcycle, how you sit in relation to the handlebars is even more critical. Even though I don't plan to race Chopper One, or even ride anywhere close to its full 1,300-horsepower potential, it was important that my seating position and access to the controls be optimized for a safe ride. My primary concern is to be able to maintain control of the bike should I decide to unleash some of its awesome power, and to be comfortable when I'm cruising it.

When designing the integrated tank/seat/fender body, I designed the seat location to fall exactly where the factory Boss Hoss seat was. If you ever have a chance to ride a Boss Hoss, you'll find that once you get past the intimidation factor of the big engine, it's a very well-balanced, fun-to-ride bike. Having the seat in the factory location would help to convey this rideability to Chopper One as long as I could bend a set of handlebars to provide sufficient reach, clear the induction system, and give me that chopper look.

The Handlebars

Finding a set of aftermarket bars was not an option. Extreme accessories such as a set of Boss Hoss ape-hangers simply do not exist. So, like most of the parts for Chopper One, I would have to make them. The main difference between the bars for Chopper One and most aftermarket sets, aside from the overall size, is the bar diameter. The standard diameter for chopper bars is 1 inch, whereas the Boss Hoss bars are 1.25 inches. From a design perspective, it's important to remember that the front end is the dynamic part of the bike; the forks must be capable of turning from

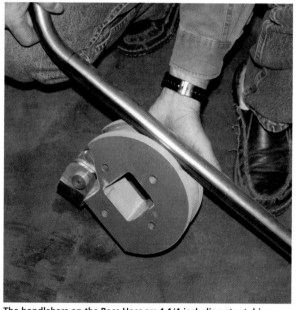

The handlebars on the Boss Hoss are 1 1/4-inch diameter tubing, and we did not have a mandrel for this size tubing. This meant we had to fabricate one. Making a mandrel turned out to be much more difficult than actually making the handlebars, but now we have one.

lock to lock without interference. The Chopper One bars have the additional obstacle of the induction system, so the actual margin for error in my bends will be close to none. Once the bars were bent to shape, they would be sent out to Sheffield Platers for a unique nickel plating finish.

With the extended handlebars measuring nearly 12 inches longer per side, all of the bar-mounted controls would likewise have to be lengthened. The throttle control on a motorcycle is a mechanism that converts the rotary motion from twisting the grip into linear motion of pulling a cable. The linkage at the throttle plate then converts the

There were only four bends involved in the bars. We use a bend program that lets you mark where each of the bends start and how much tubing you will need for a set of bends.

The main bars are 1 1/4-inch diameter, but the controls for motorcycles are only 1-inch, so a section of 1-inch tubing had to be pounded into the end of the bars and then welded in place.

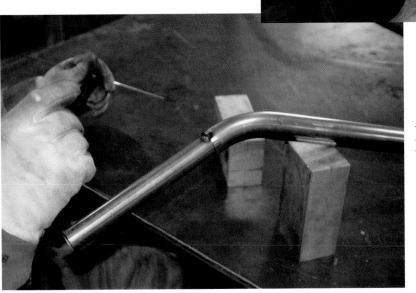

The bars were propped up to keep the end from bending as we welded them in place. The seam was TIG welded 360 degrees.

The bars had to be wide enough to clear the air scoop, two superchargers and the tank. A set of bars like this can't be ordered, so the only choice was to make them. The complete set of bars took just a few hours to bend and weld.

linear pull into rotary motion again as the carburetor's plates are opened and closed. Piecing together a throttle linkage may not seem like a big deal, but it's definitely not something to take lightly with over 1,000 horsepower on tap! If you've ever had a throttle stick, you know what I mean.

The ends of the 1.25-inch handlebars were stepped down to a 1-inch grip section that was welded to the ends of the larger tubing after the bends were made. This would allow the use of any universal-fit throttle and grip, as well as mirror brackets and brake levers. I started with a standard twist-grip mounted on the custom-made handlebars and measured the path that the cable would travel down to the carburetor. To this measurement, I added about 12 additional inches to prevent the cable from kinking or binding at any point along the path. Then I measured the amount of pull as the throttle is rotated from full off to full on. This also must be a fairly precise measurement, since damage to the cable end could occur if the carburetor linkage stops before the twist grip does. The main objective is to get the proper end length at the carburetor so that

After the bike was complete and the bars nickel plated, we added some cable holders to help keep the cables close to the bars.

Controls and Wiring—How to Make it all Work

Unless you get a handle on the tubes and wires, wiring a bike can become a real mess in no time. Try to keep things neat and organized. Being neat will also help if you need to trace a line down for repair.

the amount of twist on the grip is in synch with the carb linkage. A couple of custom throttle linkage brackets were required for Chopper One due to its unique induction system. I find it absolutely necessary to have a consistent "feel" of power each and every time the grip is twisted. Helping to achieve this are the strength of the brackets, which should not flex or move whenever the throttle is applied. A fail-safe return spring attached to the throttle lever on the carburetor is another mandatory component of the throttle linkage. The spring must mount directly to the lever of the throttle plate to eliminate any possibility of the throttle sticking in the wide-open position if the cable should bind or break. A second spring should also be installed to serve as a backup. The tension of both springs combined should be enough to pull the throttle lever back to the closed position while still allowing smooth operation of the twist grip.

The Cockpit

To the car buff, gauges are like visual portals to the inner workings of the engine. Awareness of a motorcycle's vital

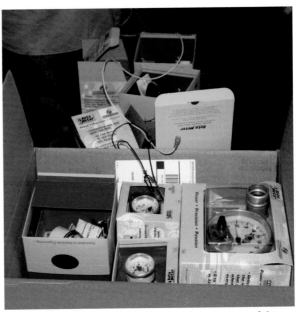

Auto Meter was our gauge of choice. I use them on many of the movie cars I build. The C2-style gauges have blue backlighting that really sets Chopper One off at night.

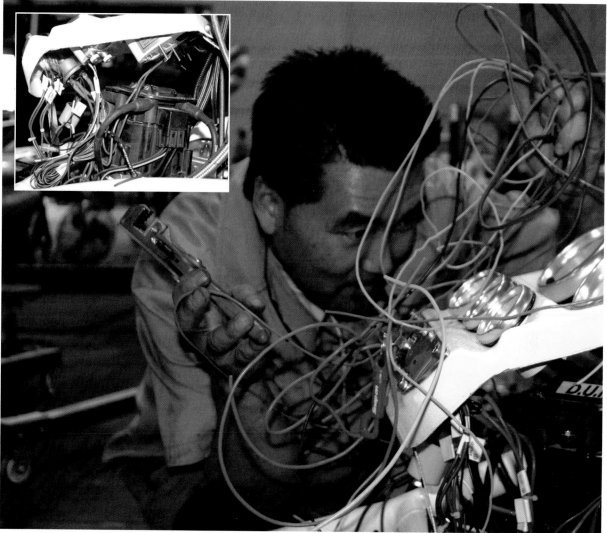

During the build the wiring looks pretty scary but this is just the first assembly and allows us to figure out what length they will be trimmed down to. Everything will be tie wrapped and organized as the final assembly is started.

Engine plumbing is an area where you do not want to cut corners as many of these tubes carry nitrous or fuel and you do not want either of those to leak in your face while traveling at a high rate of speed.

statistics are equally important, but more often than not, the functions that are monitored by gauges are usually limited to speed, engine rpm and, if you're lucky, fuel level. All other mechanical alerts are conveyed by the ubiquitous "dummy" light. For stock, daily-driver bikes, the standard speedo/tach/warning light cluster is probably more than adequate to keep you in a good running state, but the Boss Hoss, is a different animal. The Boss Hoss power plant is a purebred high-performance engine straight out of the GM Performance Parts catalog. Although no less reliable than any other motorcycle engine, the Boss Hoss is well deserving of the attention and precision monitoring that a full array of gauges provide.

As with any high-performance V-8 engine, oil pressure and water temperature are two absolute essential functions to keep a vigilant watch over. A sudden drop in oil pressure or rise in water temperature indicates a serious problem that will lead to catastrophic failure if unattended. The factory "dashboard" mounted on the Boss Hoss fuel tank includes a display of gauges for speed, oil pressure, water temperature, volts and fuel level. The faces of the stock gauges displays the Boss Hoss logo, but the gauge mechanisms are top-

Controls and Wiring—How to Make it all Work

We quickly started running out of dash space, so the fuel pressure gauge had to be mounted directly onto the fuel regulator.

The plastic vacuum-formed dash uses three brackets and is mounted to the frame so the tank can be removed without having to disassemble the dash first.

Eddie Paul's Extreme Chopper Building

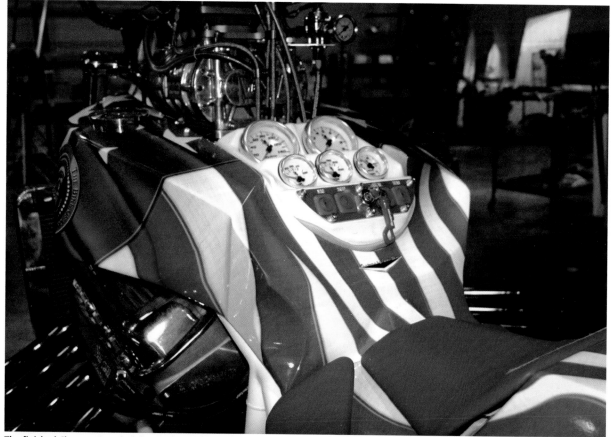

The finished Chopper One dash houses Auto Meter's C2 line of gauges that monitor speed, engine RPM, oil pressure, voltage and water temperature. The starter button on the Boss Hoss handlebar grip control was eliminated in favor of an automotive-stle key switch.

The gas cap is added and blends in nicely with the flat top of the tank.

N.O.S. nitrous lines, the main fuel line and the Holley throttle linage were all neatly routed under the tank and dash assembly.

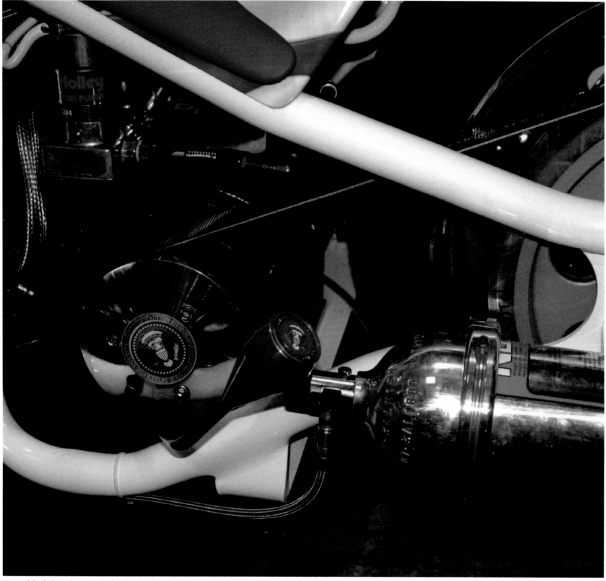

We added the nitrous tanks to the bottom rear rails and snuck the jockey shift out between the frame rail and the belt drive.

quality units made by Auto Meter. Auto Meter makes a wide assortment of gauge types, sizes and styles. By my experience, the more money I have invested in my engine, the more gauges I tend to use. To meter the operation of Chopper One, I selected Auto Meter's "C2" line with a white face and backlit illumination. I highly recommend a visit to the Auto Meter Web site for more detailed information on gauges.

The factory gauge panel will not be used with the new Chopper One tank; I designed the new tank with an open space just behind the superchargers where I could locate all of the gauges as well as indicator lights and switches. The factory location of the Boss Hoss ignition switch is at knee level below the left side of the tank with a starter button on the right-hand grip like most motorcycles. I decided to swap this setup for an automotive-type starter switch and eliminate the button.

The new housing for the instrument cluster was made of white ABS plastic. The shape was first created from a block of wood with the size and layout of each gauge taken into consideration. I placed the tach and speedo at the top with two rows for the smaller gauges right below. Rather than keeping the housing flat, I shaped special pods for the small gauges that angled upwards for easy viewing. I left just enough space below the gauges for a small panel where I would install the ignition switch, headlight and taillight switches, and nitrous arming switch.

When the wood pattern matched the shape of the dash that I wanted, I placed it onto the platform of my vacuum-former. Since this was a small piece, I was able to use my small machine, which forms with a quarter sheet (2 x 4-foot) of plastic. The dash was highly contoured, so I was able to use thin 1/16-inch ABS and still have a fairly rigid part.

I kept the entire wiring schematic of Chopper One to a very simple layout. Brian handled the design of the electrical system that consists of a small fuse block mounted to the battery box. The wires running to the rear lights were

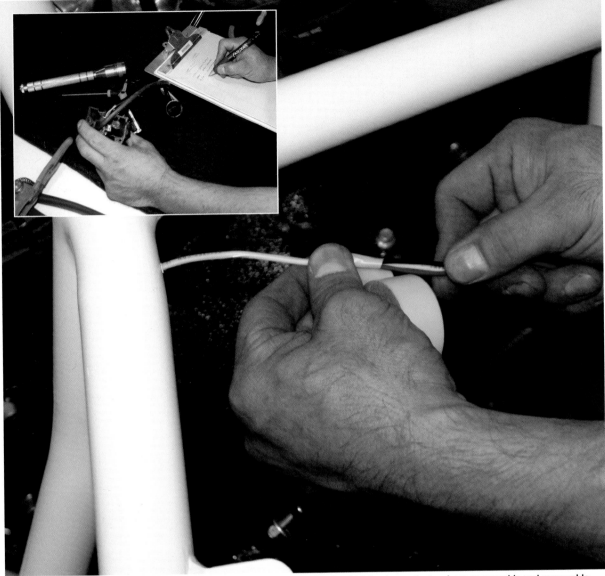

No matter how careful you are, there always seems to be one wire you missed, which is why we test and retest; assemble and reassemble.

concealed within the frame tubes to keep the rear section as clean as possible, while all other wiring is protected in white flexible wire looms. Using white looms helps to disguise the exposed wiring since the frame will also be white. Using the dimensions provided by Auto Meter, I cut out the openings for each of the C2 gauges with a hole saw. Motorcycles are notorious for vibration, so I fitted each of the gauges with an O-ring that would help to isolate them from the solid-mounted panel. Loctite Threadlocker Blue was applied on the mounting bracket bolts to make sure that everything remains in place.

The type and size of the brake system is largely dependant on the weight of the vehicle and the type of driving/riding that you'll be doing. Although I'll have an endless supply of horsepower on tap, I know that most of my riding on Chopper One will be kept to the speed limits on the street. On those rare occasions that I might twist the throttle all the way, I feel confident enough with the existing brake setup to bring me to a halt. I may be close to doubling

the power output of the engine, but in building my new hardtail frame and tank, I effectively reduced the overall weight of the bike by approximately 350 lbs. The factory Boss Hoss brakes are made by Brembo and feature two four-piston calipers up front with 12.6-inch floating discs, and a single four-piston caliper and disc at the rear. It doesn't get much better than this.

The front brakes required only the lengthening of the hydraulic line to the bar-mounted lever, but since the rear caliper was mounted to the swing arm, some custom brackets were in order. I simplified the system a bit by eliminating the line-lock "emergency brake" add-on, as well as the bolt-on brake cylinder mounting plate. Instead, I welded a plate directly onto the frame, which allowed me to shorten the rear hydraulic line. I also had to fabricate a steel lock plate that would keep the rear caliper from rotating with the disc when the brake was applied.

I thought this would be one of the cleanest ways to add a set of tail lights to the rear of the bike. Finding nice ways to put ends on tubes can be tricky on motorcycles.

Adding studs to the bottom of the gas tank was simple enough. We made sure to add Loctite to the threads.

I added tabs to the frame and aligned them with the studs on the tank for a simple way to bolt the tank to the bike.

Multi-colored wire is the best way to wire a bike if everything is going to be run internally. If you are not going to hide the wires in the frame, you may want to wire it in the color of the bike.

Wire terminal ends are sold in sets for a few dollars, and well worth having if you consider the cost of running to the hardware store for one terminal.

I placed the fuse block under the seat where it would be hard to see, but easy to access.

The throttle mount was fabricated out of a bar of aluminum and placed on the base of the carburetor.

Be sure to mount the electric fuel pump with the motor above the pump. If the pump leaks, you don't want it to leak down onto the electric motor.

For Chopper One, the mounting pan for the seat was complicated and required templates made of clear Vivac so I could see through the pattern as I laid it out.

The best seat in the house

In the world of choppers, custom seat fabrication is an art in itself. If you know how to craft with leather, sew and have your own machine, you can do it yourself. If not, then you'll either have to pay the price to have one made or be content with an off-the-shelf aftermarket seat. Once you're faced with the cost of out-sourcing this task, you'll soon realize why chopper seats are big business.

From the beginning of the Chopper One project, I knew that the seat would have to be as unique. The actual design didn't really hit me until we were almost finished with the build. All of my cars are equipped with aftermarket Recaro seats simply because I love their fit and feel. It's just a shame that they don't make anything for motorcycles. So right then and there I knew what kind of seat Chopper One really needed—the very first custom-made/aftermarket Recaro chopper seat!

To accomplish this I contacted my good friends at Recaro to get ahold of just enough of their special material to cover a small seat. My only requirements were that the material had to be red to follow Chopper One's patriotic theme, and the material had to come stitched with the familiar

The Vivac is cut out and the shape transferred to foam core, which is then cut out and used as a fitting pattern, providing the depth that the plastic does not give. This new depth will replicate the carpet that will be added to the back of the sheet metal pan.

Much of the design and pattern making was done in AutoCad, giving me better control over the total design.

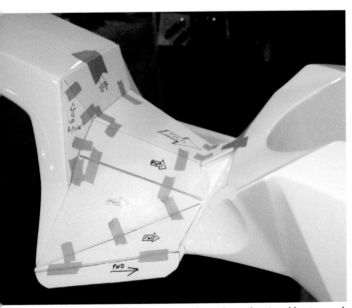

With all the sections cut out and taped together, I could get a good feel for how things will eventually look.

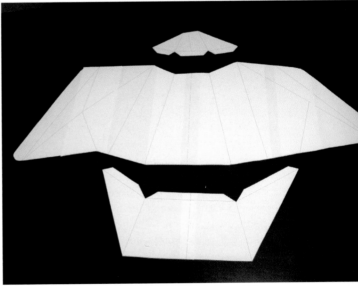

The seat eventually evolved into a three-piece design, which was definitely easier and helped us meet our deadline.

The seat pan edges were covered with a bead of plastic to keep the sharp edges of the steel from cutting the material.

The rear foam was shaped and glued onto the rear section of the pan.

Bar Enterprises used a set of shapers and trimmers for the basic shaping of the seat. The seat is definitely not a chunk of foam stuffed into the leather and stapled shut. Making a seat of this quality requires talent and some artistic ability.

Recaro logo. Then I contacted Andy at Bar Enterprises in Sunland, California. Bar Enterprises specializes in making custom seats for motorcycles. I asked him if it would be any problem for him to come up with a seat for Chopper One using the material supplied by Recaro. His answer was the kind that I like: "No problem!"

The pan, or baseplate, is the foundation that the seat is built around and should be made from a heavy gauge aluminum or steel. Some pans however, are now being made out of vacuum-formed plastic and they hold up quite well. Fiberglass is also an option. Whatever material you decide to use, before you send it out to be covered it should have the mounting brackets already attached to it or a method of attaching them to the base plate after it is covered.

The filler, or foam, is the padding that defines the contour, look and comfort level of the seat. A combination of foam densities can be used to achieve the desired feel.

The design for a good-looking custom seat may or may not be incorporated into the lines of the tank and rear fender. Good, original ideas are hard to come by. Dumb ideas are easy. Take your time if you want to design your own seat because it's something that you'll have to live and sit with when the bike is done. Being an inventor, I always

A Bosch foam rubber cutter is used to carefully cut the proper chamfer to the edges of the foam.

Recaro does not make seats for motorcycles, but we thought they should, so we did it for them.

The main piece of equipment needed for making seats is a CONSEW sewing machine. I picked one up for about $150 a few years back. It's really not that expensive to get into seat making, it just takes about 1,000 years of practice.

ask myself some basic questions whenever I try to come up with a design.

1 Has it been done before? If not, why?

2 Is it easy to do?

3 Will it cost too much?

4 Is it an improvement in safety, comfort or manufacturing, or will it just be cheaper?

5 Can you protect it by a copyright or patent, or do you need to?

Being able to translate your ideas and mental images onto paper is a big help in the process of designing. You must have the ability to make a few straight lines and a few simple curves on a piece of paper, or have an artistic friend that you can do it for you. This isn't always necessary when you do a lot of your own work, but if you want someone else to create from your design then a visual aid is a must. You will need to have the concept or idea in some form of art.

I love making patterns out of plastic or cardboard because with a pattern you are never committed to a design. You can kind of see what you want in shape and form and easily change it if you don't like it. A cut here, an extra piece taped on there and you can make a bland seat into an exciting one. Cardboard and foam core (thick paper with a sheet

A center line drawn in chalk is used as a guide to keep the logo centered and the seams aligned with each other. This will rub off when the seat is finished.

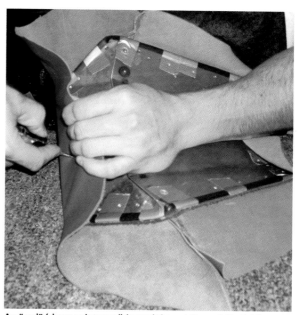

An "awl" (sharp pointy tool) is used the get through the leather so the pop-rivets can be inserted and fastened down holding the material in place. You can see the pre-drilled holes around the perimeter of the seat pan.

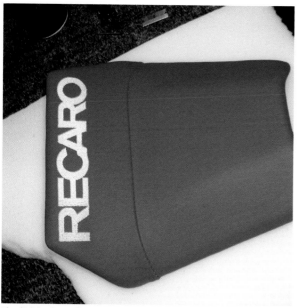

The finished seat for Chopper One is set aside for install on the bike after assembly. For this bike I wanted a thinner foam pad. The bike will only go about 25 miles before needing fuel, so comfort is not a big issue.

patterns. Then I transfer the plastic pattern to a piece of foam core, which I then cut out and tape to the bike seat area. The next piece of the pattern is outlined and cut, then taped to the last as I move across the entire seat area. Now this may sound somewhat time consuming and awkward, but I have found it to be just the opposite. With the pattern created in sections, I can make slight corrections as I move along, because if the clear plastic does not fit perfectly, I can make a small note on the plastic showing the correction to make before transferring the dimensions to foam core. The ability to move an edge or make the entire piece larger is an enormous advantage when making patterns.

When the pattern is complete you will need to mark it up so you will know how it goes back together, then you will need to take it apart so the shape can be transferred to sheet metal. Marking it will allow you to put the metal back together in the same form as the pattern. You can even mark the metal up as you cut the pieces with notes, changes, ideas, etc. One idea is to put an "A" in one corner and mark the contiguous corners with the same "A," then make another corner with a "B" and its contiguous corners with "B's."

Now, how do you mount it to the bike?

Mounting the seat on the Secret Weapon bike was easy. The bike was bolted together and it had two bolts near the seat area, anyway, so all I had to do was make a strap and utilize the existing bolts for mounting the seat. Chopper One was a bit different and I had many choices: bolts, hooks, magnets, Velcro, screws or glue.

I decided to make a silhouette of the seat out of cardboard and tape it to the seat pan. This way the upholsterers could know what I have in mind when they were shaping the seat foam.

of thin Styrofoam sandwiched between) are nice pattern materials with a very similar thickness for spacing the pan above the area you want the seat to fit. And remember: the pan needs some room under it for the cover material to wrap around

Making a pan pattern is simple and only requires a few tools, such as an X-acto knife, a straight edge, felt tip marker and a square, along with a roll of tape.

I generally start in the center of any pattern and work my way outward. I sometimes work with both clear plastic and cardboard pattern material. The plastic I use is in very thin sheets and allows me to see through it as I make the

I changed the design from a one-piece to a three-piece, after considering the amount of work and what is called "accumulation of error." By breaking the seat down into three parts we had fewer bends per section and less error in total measurements or bends.

The seat cover can be anything from basic black vinyl or leather to any number of custom materials. Of course, I chose to use Recaro seat material, but, depending on the application, you might want marine-grade vinyl, alligator skin, or your pet dog, if it feels good to you. For durability and prolonged exposure to the elements, consider a waterproof covering or European leather. Piping can be added along the seams for style, or a logo or even a design of your choice if you supply the art to the upholsterer.

If you're sending your pan out to be upholstered, write notes and instructions directly on the pan. This way the upholsterer will not lose them and you can prove you made the notes with a digital photo of the seat that you should include with your order. I had Bar Enterprises come out to the shop to see the bike and get an idea of what we were building before they started on the seat. This way they could get the real feel for what I was trying to convey in the overall theme of the bike. This helped, and due to the time constraints on the project, they agreed to jump right on this project and get it turned around as fast as they could and get it back to me

Also, if you contract somebody to do a job for you, trust him or her with it. Don't tell the upholsterer how

The bottom of the seat had Velcro sewn on with a matching side that will double stick to the body of the bike. This was only to hold each section in place as we drilled holes for the permanent mounting brackets.

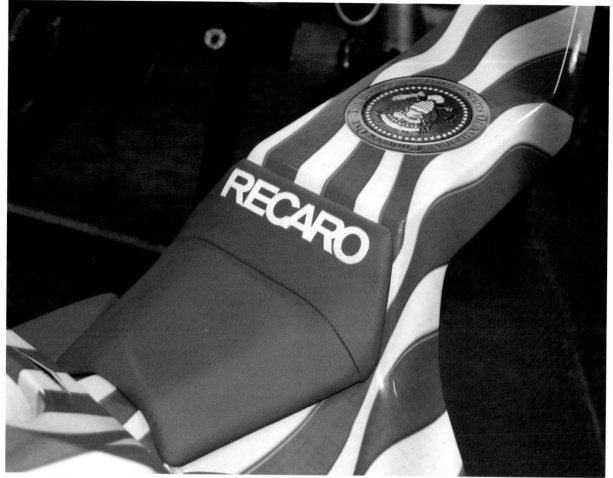

You won't find a seat like this in any bike shop. This is the one and only Recaro prototype chopper seat.

to make your seat. You can let them know what you want and then leave them alone. In my shop, I draw the line when someone starts telling me how to build their car. I prefer they let me know what they want and then go home. You've seen those funny signs with escalating prices based on your watching and helping. Well, they are not a joke. If you see one, that means the business doesn't want you hanging around and getting in the way.

Once the seat comes back, install it as soon as you can so you know right away if there is a problem. I have put things away and not checked them until I needed them, and then found they do not fit or something was wrong. Because I waited too long to check it out, I could not get it covered under any kind of warranty.

I put a lot of effort into the design and execution of seat making because it's the most important factor in making my ride a comfortable one.

Chapter Six

Molding and Finishing

Al Cadena preps the completed frame for molding by sandblasting. This is the best way to insure a contamination-free surface for the filler to adhere to.

The final phase of the Chopper One build-up includes all of the things that will make this bike look really extreme. In this chapter, we'll discuss how the tank and frame were meticulously prepped, molded, and painted, followed by a blow-by-blow of the complete assembly of the entire bike. We'll also take a look at the increasingly popular art of vinyl graphics with Troy Downey and his crew at APE Wraps. There is no substitute for the intricate detail and infinite color effects that can be produced by an expert painter and his or her spray gun. On the other hand, vinyl offers some very noteworthy advantages that no painter can match.

Molding the frame

Whenever I think about molding the frame of a chopper, I can't help but reminisce about the old days of mixing up can after can of plastic filler and sanding my fingers to the bone. Piles upon piles of grated shavings and filler dust would get swept into a dark corner of my cobwebbed garage, and as the pile grew higher, I knew that I was getting progressively closer to what I was envisioning as the finished product. Sure, I could have just shot a bit of paint on the frame and called it a day; but then anyone could have done that. Customizing is all about individuality. I like to create things that make people stop and wonder how I made it. And when people see the things that I create and ask me how I did it, I always try to take the time to explain.

A frame with its welds exposed will look fine with just a simple coat of basic black paint on it providing, of course, that the welds are nice. This is pretty much what you get with a factory motorcycle frame. Whether frame molding came about as a way to hide sloppy welds or to simply make the frame look good is unknown, but the fact is, it accomplishes both. Although the welding on Chopper One's frame was pretty close to presentation quality, I still wanted to smooth things out before painting. No chopper can rightfully be classified as a custom without some molding on the frame.

Every area of this bike had gone through progressive steps and the frame molding was no exception. We started by taking the completed frame and lightly grinding the welded joints in preparation for the filler. This was not as simple as it sounds, because if you overdo this aspect of the job you could easily compromise the strength of the frame

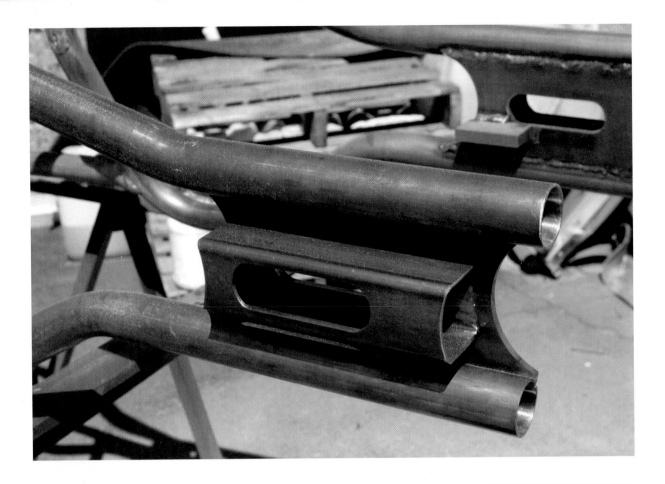

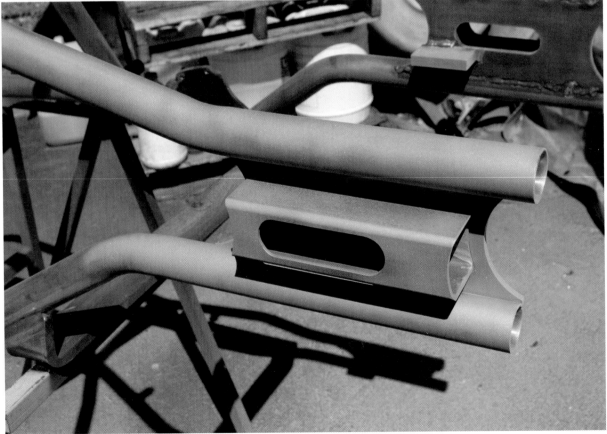

Here is the rear axle section of the frame before and after sandblasting.

The chemistry of molding

Plastic filler is the mainstay of auto body repair work. Without it, even the simplest door ding couldn't be fixed with any degree of cost-efficiency. Plastic fillers were developed to take the place of lead, which for all practical purposes, is now a lost art. There are some long-standing misconceptions about the use of plastic filler that I feel need to be put to rest. First of all, "Bondo," which is plastic filler, is actually a trade name of the Bondo Corporation and not a generic term, even though many people use it as such. There are several companies that manufacture top-quality plastic fillers, including Evercoat, the brand that I use exclusively in my shop. The second issue concerns quality, something that all of us strive for. To sum it up: Plastic filler will last the life of the car as long as it is applied correctly over a properly prepared surface.

Plastic filler is a polyester-based substance that requires the addition of a catalyst for it to harden. The amount of catalyst can vary depending on ambient temperature, so the best way to determine the proper ratio is to mix up a small test batch and note the shade of color of the catalyzed mix. If you use different brands of filler, you'll notice that the color of the catalyst might be red or blue. A colored catalyst provides a visual indicator that tells when your filler and catalyst are thoroughly mixed. When a batch is mixed, the mixture should have a uniform color with no swirls. In my experience, there is no difference between the different catalyst colors, with one exception: The red catalyst has a tendency to bleed through primer and sealer coats and discolors the final finish of certain light colors. So as a general rule, I avoid using red catalyst with plastic filler.

Plastic filler has improved by leaps and bounds over the years. The Evercoat line of fillers offers easy sanding with minimal build-up and clogging on the sandpaper. We use their Z-Grip for general purpose work, Extreme Rage for covering slight imperfections, Metal Glaze for filling those tiny pinholes and sanding scratches, and Everglass for rust-sensitive areas. Everglass is a waterproof fiberglass-reinforced filler that is both stronger and harder than standard filler.

Once you get into working with plastic filler, you'll find that you can get quite creative with it. We did a simple molding job on the Chopper One frame, but like any form of customizing, you're limited by nothing but your imagination. You can also find other related uses for plastic filler. Way back in the old days when molding Harley-Davidson frames, I often finished a neck area on a frame and then carved an intricate design into the filler. I would then cover the molded neck with a coat of mold release or wax and then, using body filler as a casting material, I would make a casting of the newly fabricated neck design. The next time I needed to mold a neck I would only have to clamp the mold onto the neck and inject a batch of filler into the mold, and within minutes I had an intricately carved or shaped neck area in a fraction of the time it took to mold the original neck. I kept the molds in my tool box and never told anyone about them until now, so, if your bike was one of the frames I molded in this manner, then you now know how I did it so fast. I could mold an entire frame in a half a day as long as it was a Harley frame. As I always say, inventors are often more lazy than smart.

at the weld. The person who handles the grinding chores should be the same person that did the welding, or at least has a good idea of how it was welded. To maintain the structural integrity of the frame, you must be familiar with how it was constructed, and being aware of the different types of weld joints such as lap welds, butt welds, surface welds, plug welds, etc., is a big help during the grinding process.

One way to prep a frame for molding and painting is to have it sandblasted. Sandblasting is a fast way to remove rust, layers of old paint or similar build-up on parts such as a motorcycle frame. Properly sandblasted, a motorcycle frame is left with a perfect surface for applying plastic filler or undercoats such as primer. A sandblaster utilizes a high-velocity flow of air from a compressor to project grains of sand onto a surface. The force with which the sand particles hit the surface determines how deep the grain will penetrate through the material that you want removed. The type of blasting media also determines the degree of material removal. A sandblasted surface has a very clean but irregular texture that has the ability to grab and lock the filler onto it. If you have a smooth surface with very few irregularities, filler will not stick well. Sandblasting also offers the advantage of getting into tight spots where a grinding disc cannot reach.

Grinding is accomplished with either an electric, or pneumatic grinder and a reinforced abrasive wheel. For lighter grinding requirements, a coated abrasive disc is used with grits ranging from a coarse 16-grit to 40-grit. Finer grits than this tend to leave the surface a little too smooth for adequate filler adhesion. For shaping plastic filler, sandpaper is used instead of discs. Typical grits for working with filler range from 36 grit and get progressively finer up to 80 grit. Once you have plastic filler worked to

It's good to have a large worktable since the frame will have to be maneuvered around quite a bit.

The Evercoat Z-Grip filler is applied to all of the welded joints. Because of the tight angles and curves, applying and sanding of the filler must be done by hand.

The cheese-grater is Brian's cheapest and most effective tool for working plastic filler. Accurate rough-shaping with the grater is the key to fast, straight bodywork.

The half-round cheese grater works well for the inner tank cutout because it matches the radius very well and will make short work of the shaping process.

a level surface in 80-grit, it is then ready for paint prep. Brian handles all of the major shaping and molding tasks in my shop, and the first tool that he uses for shaping filler is known in the surfboard industry as a Sureform file. In the automotive field we call it a "cheese-grater." A cheese-grater is similar to a file but with a cutting face like an actual cheese-grater. In the right hands, this little tool can work wonders and save an extraordinary amount of time, not to mention the cost of sandpaper. In the wrong hands, though, it can be a tool of destruction and waste due to its fast material-cutting ability.

The molding of the Chopper One frame was performed by Brian Hatano and Alfonso Cadena. Al is a machine operator who wants to get more into the specialized field of custom fabrication work. This was a perfect opportunity for Al to acquire some on-the-job training in working with plastic filler. At a shop like mine, we need people who can both mold and shape metal. Someone capable of taking any job all the way through from start to finish is a rarity in this industry and I'm fortunate to have one of the few who can. Under Brian's tutoring, Al performed his very first molding job on the Chopper One frame with excellent

The grater is also used for cutting the lines straight. The tank will get completely roughed into shape before the sanding blocks are brought out.

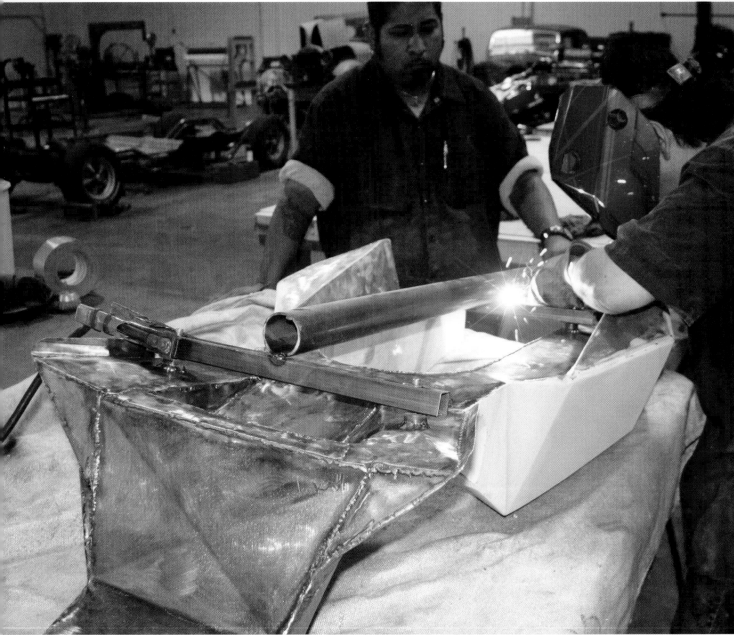

Our standard tank stands could not accommodate the custom Chopper One piece, so it was necessary to build a custom holder to continue work.

results. The process started with a light grinding around the welds, followed by a thorough blasting with a hand-held sandblaster. The sand that we used for this was common "sandbox sand" available from any home improvement center. This left Al with clean, bare metal to begin applying our Evercoat fillers to.

Coarse-cutting with 36-grit is the first stage of sanding after shaping plastic filler with the cheese-grater. The best way to mold a bike is in the progressive order of the sandpaper grits (grater, 36, 80, 180, etc). Medium-cut sanding is the same as the rough, except you are using finer-grit sandpaper. As the grits get finer, you should be doing less shaping and more smoothing. If you have to take a step back and reapply some filler in a spot or two (and this will happen), you will wind up sanding over areas that

have already been sanded smooth. This is where experience comes into play to avoid chasing a low spot or high spot over the entire area that has been filled. On Chopper One, Brian taught Al how to mold the frame, which Al got a kick out of—for the first three days, then it got to be somewhat tedious. But you can't quit until you are done and you can't skip a step or you will more than likely end up creating more work for yourself.

Prime Time

Once the entire Chopper One frame was sanded down with 80-grit, it was time to give it a coat of primer. I uses to apply primer with a spray gun only because you never knew exactly what you got in those aerosol "rattle" cans.

Guns and Ammo!

The gun is probably the most important tool for automotive painting, but there is a lot of support equipment that goes along with it. You can have the best gun in the world, but it won't spray a drop of paint without all the things connected to it.

The air compressor is the heart of the painting process. In my shop, we use two big industrial units with 10-horsepower motors and 80-gallon tanks. Pressure is regulated at 90psi throughout the shop although the system is capable of 150psi. A constant 90psi is more than adequate to operate most tools. In the spray booth, the pressure is regulated down to 60psi for most paint jobs.

The network of air lines running throughout the shop to the various work stations and to the paint booth was carefully laid out. We used 1-inch Schedule 40 PVC conduit that runs around the perimeter of the inside of the shop up along the ceiling. At each outlet, the conduit drops down 15 feet with a drain valve at the bottom to release the trapped water and an air chuck placed about 2 feet above the drain provides ample air. This is the best way to control the condensation that normally accumulates in the lines. At the end of each day, the compressors and all the petcocks are opened up to drain the moisture.

There are different types of compressors: single stage, double stage and three stage. The stages refer to the number of pistons of differing sizes that recompress the air into high pressure. As a general rule, the more stages, the higher the pressure. The cubic feet per minute, or CFM, is based on a few variables, such as PSI (pounds per square inch), the horsepower of the compressor's drive motor, the belt ratio, ambient temperature, the length, material and diameter of the conduit used in the system, and even the number of elbows and angles of the elbows (i.e. 45 degree or 90 degree). These all help determining the output pressure and flow at the nozzle. Keep in mind that a small compressor will have to run longer to produce the same amount of air as a large compressor. Therefore, the small compressor will tend to generate more heat and more condensation in the lines than a large compressor. So unless you are willing to spend some time learning the physics involved in setting up a spray system, you might want to call on a professional to advise you along the way.

Since the compressors are constantly running, we maintain them regularly to avoid problems and downtime. At home, most people run an air line directly off of the compressor. This is not a bad thing,

Paint Gun care and maintenance is extremely important. Brian cares for his guns as if they were surgical instruments! After the primer is applied, he carefully breaks the gun down and cleans it in the Hercules Gun Washer. This process is performed anytime the gun is used.

but unless the compressor must be portable, it's best to plumb your home garage much the same way that a shop does. That means running hard lines up high with vertical drop-downs and drains at every outlet.

Whether or not you intend to use an air supply for painting, you should always have a good regulator and moisture trap plumbed into the system. Air tools will run forever if the air pressure is properly regulated and the air supply is clean and dry. When painting, moisture and contamination in the air supply is the painter's worst enemy! To avoid any problems in the spray booth, we have the four-stage Devilbiss Clean Air Desiccant Air Dryer System that filters the air, removes moisture and regulates the pressure of the air. No spray booth should be without a system like this!

As wild as Chopper One is, the paint job on the frame and tank is a basic single-stage House of Kolor urethane white. It's the kind of paint job that anyone with the right equipment can do. The right equipment includes the gun—Brian recommends the Devilbiss Plus or GTi HVLP, or a Satajet—the compressor, a good desiccant filter and regulator, and a solvent-resistant 5/16 or 3/8 air hose. Many good paint jobs have been done without a spray booth, but spraying in a nice, well-lit booth can only make a good job come out better. The spray booth in my shop is a cross-flow design manufactured by Standard Tools and Equipment. And behind the double-doors is where the magic of custom painting takes place.

The Chopper One tank mount had to be heavy duty. It's made of mild steel tubing and attaches to an engine stand.

Now the tank can be turned around and moved with ease for the remainder of the job.

Brian performs a trial fit of the tank to the frame.

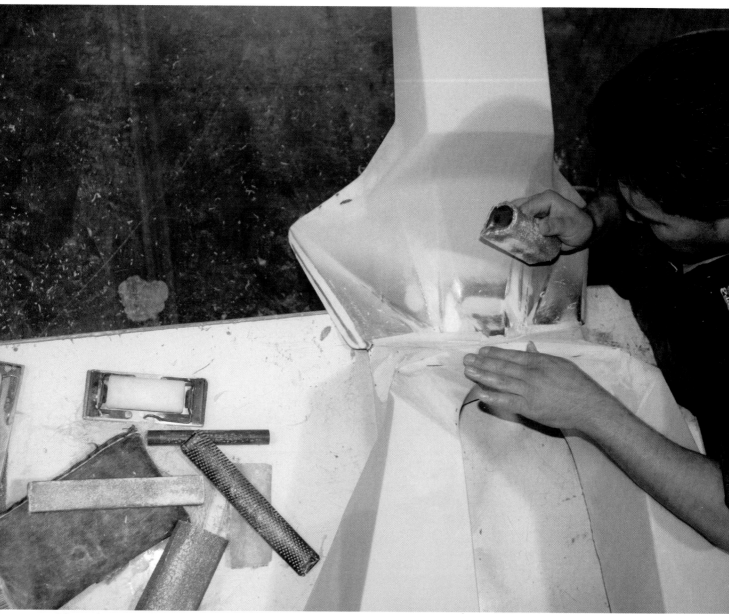

Brian used every type of sanding block in his Snap-on tool box for this job! Getting the tank smooth, straight and perfectly symmetrical takes a lot of patience and skill.

Now, there's a whole new world of aerosol undercoatings that offer the quality and fill characteristics of automotive primer with spray can convenience. Brian uses Evercoat's High-Build Primer for most applications and Acid-Etch Primer on aluminum projects or where corrosion might be an issue.

One of the more important things to keep in mind is that primer is a surfacer, as opposed to a topcoat. A surfacer is an undercoating that provides a suitable substrate for the application of sealers and paint. A sandable primer/surfacer is applied over areas that have been worked on to fill slight imperfections and sanding scratches left from the work. Techniques vary among painters, but the standing rule in our shop is to featheredge with 120-grit paper and work filler down from 36-grit to 80-grit or finer before applying primer. This reduces the possibility of problems due to sand-scratch swelling.

Twenty years ago, there was no need to elaborate on what type of primer to use. In fact, the guys in my shop always kept an old Sharp Model 75 loaded with Ditzler (now PPG) DZL-32 acrylic lacquer primer hanging off of the old painted-splattered wooden bench. We never had to clean the gun or even stir the primer in the cup because we used it so often. It was always ready and the primer was always the same no matter what we were working on or what kind of paint we would be using. There were other primers, too, but we seldom had a need for anything other than plain old lacquer primer. Some builders are still lucky enough to be able to get and use acrylic lacquer primers and paint, but here in California, the good people from the air management district have outlawed its use. What we have to work with now are catalyzed urethane and polyurethane primers, waterborne primers, and the latest aerosol primers from companies like Evercoat and SEM.

Molding and Finishing

Having worked from front to rear, the molding job is almost complete. Note the use of lead-shot bags to hold the tank in place.

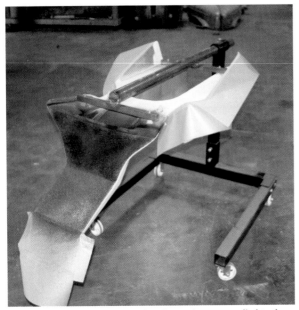

Eastwood Rust Encapsulator and Undercoating was applied to the underside of the rear fender area just prior to the application of primer.

With all of the molding complete, it was time for primer. We used Evercoat Slick Sand, a high-build, catalyzed polyester-based primer.

Brian loads his Devilbiss gun with the primer and gives both the tank and frame two coats of Slick Sand.

Paint and painting equipment have also changed greatly over the years. For the longest time, the standard spray guns of the industry were the Binks Model 7 and the Devilbiss JGA 502. These were the only two types of guns that ever saw the inside my shop's spray booth back in the '70s and '80s. Those guns are still available but now, with the mandatory use of HVLP (high volume, low pressure) guns, the old Model 7 and the JGA are obsolete.

Technically speaking, an HVLP spray gun will produce no more than 10psi through the air cap, whereas the old high-pressure spray guns produce 50psi or more. Nowadays, many areas (southern California, for instance) prohibit the use of high-pressure guns in the automotive industry, but an HVLP gun is in compliance with all such regulations. The advantages of HVLP guns are primarily environmental, since the low-pressure characteristic keeps the overspray to a minimum. Material cost is also somewhat reduced.

Another gun-related change is the evolution of the gravity-feed design. The siphon-feed (cup on the bottom) gun was pretty much the standard style. Gravity-feed (cup on the top) guns, although not new technology, have all but replaced the siphon-feed style in most shops, but not

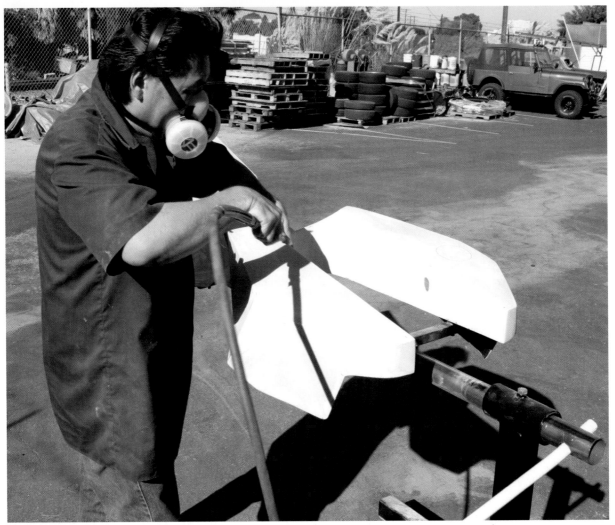

Sanding is a dusty process, so before the primer is applied the tank must be blown off thoroughly with an air nozzle.

mine. My painter, Brian (yes, he does painting, too!), uses the Devilbiss GTi with a siphon cup for all of his custom work. He occasionally uses a gravity-feed GTi as well as other gun makes such as Sata, but his favorite is the old-style cup-on-the-bottom GTi.

Another element that seems to affect the way a paint job comes out is the pressure factor. Not air pressure, but the self-imposed mental pressure that a painter puts on himself to not make mistakes. The solution to this is not an easy one. I discovered way back when I had my first custom shop that if we had a high-end custom paint job to do, my best painters would sometimes make mistakes that a beginner might do—things like dragging the air hose against the side of the car. But less critical paint jobs like those that we do for the movie studios always seem to come out great. I realized that the big difference was the painter's "state of mind" before and during the paint job. The custom job had to be perfect, so the painter went in the booth with the added stress. But on the movie job, the paint jobs were usually flawless, and they did not have to be since the camera hides flaws.

The point to my rambling here is to relax and think about the fact that no matter what goes wrong in the paint booth, it can easily be fixed.

Another short story to illustrate this point: My dad had this old Dodge that he painted. When he was done, the neighbors all wanted him to paint their cars because his Dodge came out flawless. The funny thing was, my dad did not have a spray booth or even a spray gun back then, just a bucket of paint and a brush. Oh yeah, some sandpaper and a lot of rubbing compound! His "perfect" paint job was actually the result of many hours of hard labor, color sanding, and rubbing, rather than skill with a gun. The fact is that you can color-sand and rub out almost any superficial flaw in the paint.

Paint prep is the most important phase of any paint job. I've heard some painters break the importance of it down into mathematics. "Preparation is 90 percent of a good paint job." Or, "A paint job is two-thirds sanding and cleaning, and one-third spraying." Of course, it doesn't really matter what percentage of the job is what, just suffice it to say that good preparation is important.

The prep stage begins after the molding of all the parts is complete and in primer. For Brian, this was actually a very routine job since the color for both the frame and tank is a single-stage basic white. My plan was to carry the red, white

After the two coats of primer are applied, a light mist of black paint is sprayed over the tank and frame. This is called a "guide coat." As its name implies, the guide coat will show where any low spots or imperfections exist by leaving a trace of black after sanding.

Starting with 180-grit on a sanding block, the tank must be block-sanded and primed no less than three times before it is ready for paint. The final block sanding will be done with either 320-grit dry paper or 600-grit wet-or-dry.

More sanding! The tank is shaping up as the sandpaper grits get progressively finer.

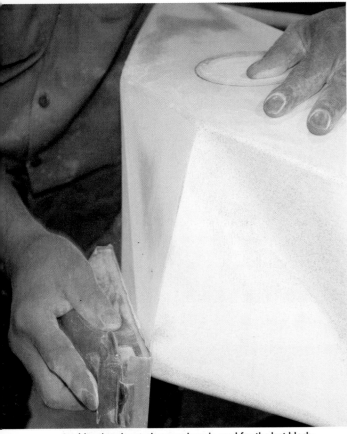

A white-tinted waterborne primer is used for the last block-sanding. We choose to dry-sand the tank with 320.

and blue theme out with a white frame and American flag graphics on the tank and fender. I know that flag graphics are nothing new, but what is new is the way I planned to apply the graphics.

The inspiration for the flag design is rather unique. In fact, it was sitting right in front of me for the longest time. The mouse pad that I have for my desktop computer has a flag on it. I picked it up at the store simply because I like the red, white and blue. Little did I know at the time that the design on the $2 pad would someday grace the flanks of the world's most insane chopper!

Vinyl Wraps:
The Alternative To Paint

While Brian laid a perfect coat of white urethane on the frame, tank and fender, I was busy scanning my mouse pad into my computer so that I could manipulate the design onto the tank with the PhotoShop and Illustrator software programs. Although we could carry the whole graphics scheme out from start to finish in custom paint, I was still faced with a pending deadline of having the bike ready to show. The process of airbrushing the red, white and blue design the way that I wanted would take the better part of a week. By comparison, laying the artwork down in vinyl could be done in an afternoon, according to Troy Downey of APE Wraps. APE, by the way, stands for "Ain't Paint

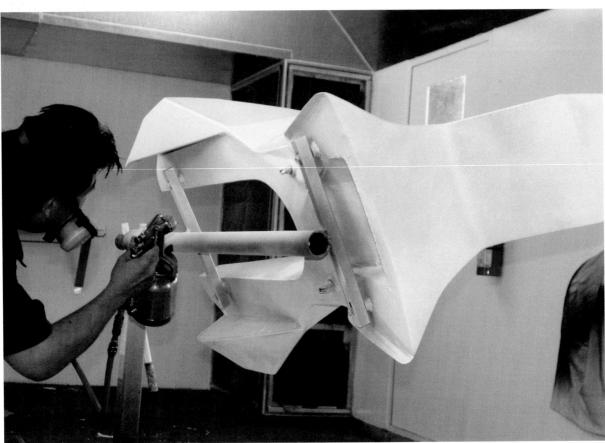

Spraying starts on the underside so that the last pass will be on the topside. This minimizes the possibility of any dry mist remaining in high-visibility areas.

Prepare To Paint

"A painter is only as good as his last paint job." It's statements like this that makes the art of painting a scary and often intimidating process for a lot of do-it-yourselfers. If this sounds like you, the feeling most likely stems from fear of the unknown. Even an experienced painter isn't always sure what the finished result is going to look like, so I can just imagine the apprehension that a novice would have. Painting scares the heck out of the best of us because as soon as the painting is complete, the painter will immediately be subjected to critique by a panel of "experts" who will inspect the quality of the finish with a microscope! One run and he will never hear the end of it; two runs and he might as well consider a new profession.

The best way to approach a paint job with the utmost confidence is to eliminate as many of the unknowns as humanly possible. This means learning the ins and outs of the spray gun, acquiring a fundamental understanding of the type of paint that you'll be using, and maybe even spraying a test panel so you'll know what to expect. Keep in mind that every type of paint exhibits a different spraying characteristic, and every substrate (spraying surface) can pose an infinite array of potential challenges or problems that will put the skill of the painter to the test. In other words, very seldom are two paint jobs ever alike unless you're spraying new cars on a production line.

Painting a bike frame is difficult because you need to constantly rotate the spray gun so it is perpedicular to the tubes' surface while maintaining a constant speed and distance from the frame.

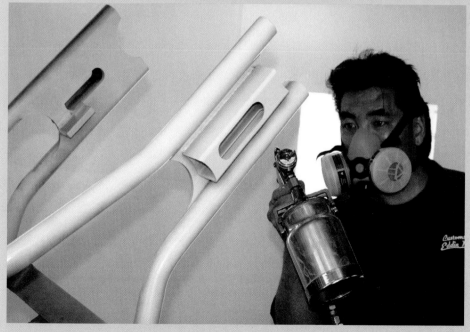

This paint job was complicated by the fact that Brian had rectangular tubes, flat plates and round tubing to contend with as he sprayed the frame with a coat of House of Kolor white urethane.

The tank is turned midway through the process. An engine stand proved to be quite handy for this.

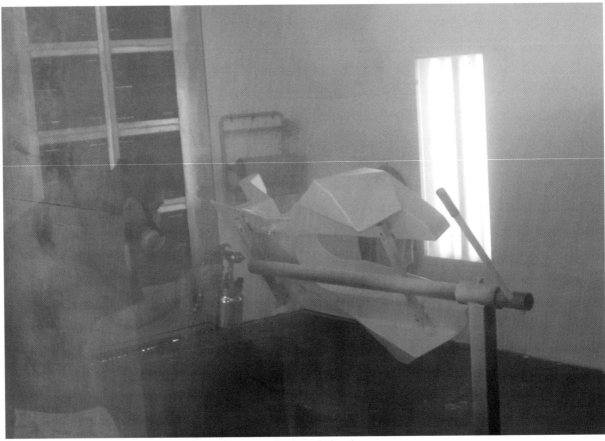

Even with the strong fan circulating the air, the urethane spray clouds up the booth.

Consistency and a steady hand is important for proper flow.

Enterprises," a pretty clever acronym for the company that literally performs miracles on everything from cars to 18-wheelers. Once I furnished Troy with a basic idea of what I wanted for the Chopper One graphics, he took the ball and ran straight for the finish line with it.

I met Troy at a San Diego car show a few years back. Once I saw what he was capable of doing with vinyl, I knew that it was just a matter of time before we were working on a project together. The general misconception that most people have about what Troy does is that they mistake vinyl for the common adhesive-backed decal. The APE Wraps vinyl is definitely *not* a sticker! In fact, Troy uses a special vinyl made by the Avery Graphics Company that is extremely durable. The Avery material is available in a wide variety of colors and effects, and the vinyl can also be custom-printed by computer.

When you consider the time-saving factor and the incredible amount of detail that a good vinyl treatment can provide, it's only natural for a painter to feel somewhat threatened by this fast-emerging new technique of refinishing. Even Brian, a custom painter with more than 20 years experience, admits that there a lot of effects that Troy and his crew can do in a very short amount of time that would take him days or weeks to do with paint. On the other hand, I don't think that anybody can dispute the fact that there is no substitute for a true custom paint job. One thing that Troy, Brian and I all agree on is that custom painting and the art of vinyl can peacefully coexist, and in

many applications, on the same vehicle!

With the Chopper One tank having so many inwardly radiused angles and sharp corners, this was a true test of Troy's wrapping skills and of the Avery Graphics vinyl's ability to conform to such an extreme shape. Apparently, Troy did not anticipate any problems because he assured me that he and his number one wrapper, Rich, could have

Molding and Finishing

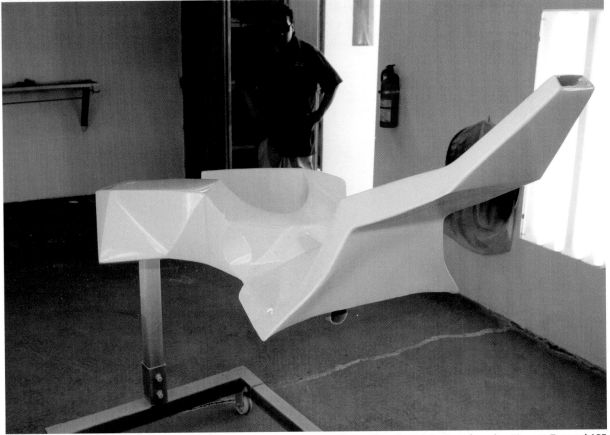

Viola! The painter stands back to admire the many hours of work nearing completion. Once the paint sets up for a day, It's up to Troy and APE Wraps to apply the finishing touches.

the graphics done in a mere two hours. The only thing that he would need is a nice, smooth paint job on the tank for the vinyl to adhere to. So knowing that absolutely no part of the paint would be visible, Brian applied a flawless coat of white to the combination tank/fender assembly and allowed it to set up for two days before the vinyl was applied.

In the meantime, Troy converted my mouse pad flag design into a beautiful piece of digital art that was printed onto a sheet of the Avery vinyl. When Troy and his crew arrived at the shop, Rich handled the Chopper One job. True to his word, the entire wrap was completed in about two hours, including the additional pseudo-Presidential seals that were applied to the sides of the tank and a few other strategic spots around the bike.

This mouse pad provided the inspiration for the graphic scheme!

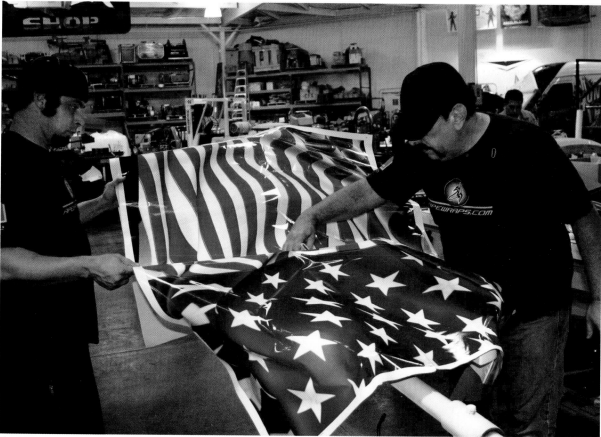

The APE Wraps crew work wonders with vinyl. It is definitely an art to place the design exactly where it should be.

Molding and Finishing

The vinyl started out looking like a wet blanket, but within minutes it started taking shape and I was soon sold on vinyl — for certain applications.

Rich is constantly pulling, stretching and repositioning the wrap until he's totally satisfied. This process is a true testament to the durability of the Avery material.

Eddie Paul's Extreme Chopper Building

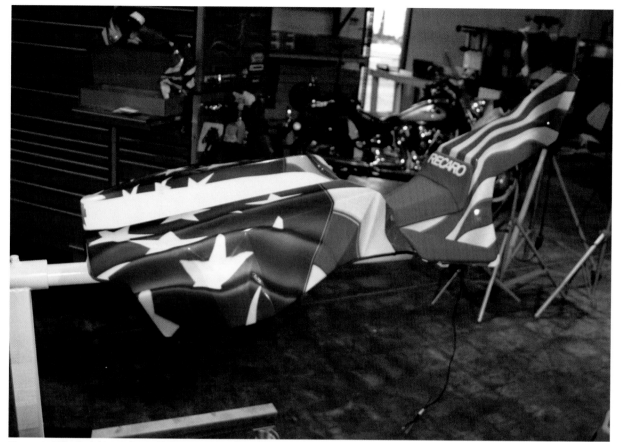

It's a wrap! The tank is complete with Recaro seat pads in place.

While the dash and Auto Meter Gauges are being installed, the final graphic touch is applied by Troy Downey of APE Wraps. It's the Chopper One seal reminiscent of the famous presidential emblem.

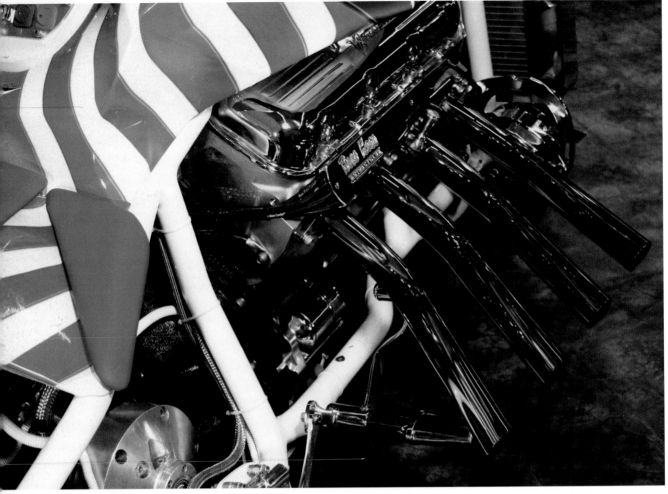

You won't see another Boss Hoss street bike with pipes like these! Highly illegal, but who cares?

I found a good place for the liquid horsepower near the back of the bike, and with a tank on each side I could have a few hundred extra ponies at the push of a button.

Is it Over?

As you can see in the photos throughout the book, my crew and I had a blast building the ultimate chopper. But as an inventor and a creator, I've had to ask myself, "Is this it? Is this really the ultimate extreme chopper? How can I possibly come up with something even more outrageous?" Rest assured that the solution to this dilemma is already formulating in my mind. I can say that it involves not one but two engines this time, and...well, the rest is a subject for another book! In the meantime, if you're looking for more in-depth reading on building, repairing, painting and general customizing, keep an eye out at your local bookstore for the next KP Books publication and my name, Eddie Paul.

A bank of Auto Meter C2 gauges reside in the vacuum-formed ABS plastic dash. The illuminated rocker switches control the lights and NOS nitrous system. The key, of course, fires the radical Boss Hoss up.

Inventor, designer, customizer, stuntman and Chopper One builder Eddie Paul atop his most extreme creation yet!

Appendix I

Manufacturer Source Guide

APE Wraps (vinyl graphics)
P.O. Box 180767
Coronado, CA 92178
1-619-435-0624
Web site: www.apewraps.com

Avery Dennison, Graphics Division, North America
  (vinyl graphics materials)
7009 Livingston Drive
Denton, TX 76210
1-888-283-7955
Web site: www.averygraphics.com

Auto Meter Competition Instruments (gauges)
Web site: www.autometer.com

3M Company (abrasives, paint prep and metal treatment)
Web site: www.3M.com

Bar Enterprises (custom motorcycle seats, leather accessories)
8127 Foothill Blvd.
Sunland, CA 91040
1-818-353-3888
Web site: www.harleyseats.com

Bend-Pak / Ranger (motorcycle and automobile lifts)
1645 Lemonwood Drive
Santa Paula, CA USA 93060
Local phone: 805-933-9970, toll-free phone: 800-253-2363
Web site: www.bendpak.com

Bessey Tools North America (clamps, snips, hammers)
1165 Franklin Blvd., Unit G / P.O. Box 490
Cambridge, ON N1R 5V5
Phone: 519-621-7240
Web site: www.americanclamping.com

Bosch Tools and Accessories (cordless and electric power tools)
Phone: 877-BOSCH-99
Web site: www.boschtools.com

Boss Hoss Motorcycles
Web site: www.bosshoss.com

Channellock, Inc. (pliers, cutters)
1306 South Main Street
Meadville, PA 16335
Phone: 800-724-3018
Web site: www.channellock.com

Chicago Pneumatic (pneumatic power tools)
Web site: www.chicagopneumatic.com

Customs By Eddie Paul (design, custom cars, motorcycles, film/
  television vehicles, paint and fabrication work, CNC machining, video
  production)
2305 Utah Avenue
El Segundo, California 90245
Phone: 310-643-8515
Web site: www.epindustries.com

Devilbiss Automotive Refinishing (painting equipment, spray guns, air
  regulators and filters)
Phone: 800-445-3988
Web site: www.autorefinishdevilbiss.com

Eagle Bending Machines (hydraulic tubing roller)
Phone: 251-937-0947
Web site: www.eaglebendingmachines.com

Earl's Performance Plumbing (braided lines, AN fittings)
Web site: www.holley.com

Eastwood Company (restoration, autobody and metal-working tools)
263 Shoemaker Road
Pottstown, PA 19464
Phone: 800-345-1178
Web site: www.eastwood.com

E. P. Industries, Inc. (metal fabrication tools)
2305 Utah Avenue
El Segundo, CA 90245
Phone: 310-245-8515
Web site: www.epindustries.com

ESAB (welding equipment and consumables)
Web site: www.esab.com

Evercoat (body fillers, primers, metal treatment, fiberglass materials)
6600 Cornell Road
Cincinnati, OH 45242
Phone: 513-489-7600
Web site: www.evercoat.com

Haulmark (motorcycle trailers)
14054 C.R. 4 E
Bristol, IN 46507
Phone: 800-348-7530
Web site: www.haulmark.com

Holley Performance Products (carburetors, electric fuel pump)
Web site: www.holley.com

House of Kolor (custom automotive paint)
210 Crosby Street

Picayune, Mississippi 39466
Phone: 601-798-4229
Web site: www.houseofkolor.com

Hutchins Mfg. Company
(pneumatic sanders and accessories)
49 North Lotus Avenue
Pasadena, CA 91107
Phone: 626-792-8211
Web site: www.hutchinsmfg.com

Hypertherm, Inc. (plasma cutters)
Web site: www.hypertherm.com

Ingersoll Rand (pneumatic power tools)
Web site: www.irtools.com

Innova—Emissive Energy Corp. (L.E.D. flashlights)
135 Circuit Drive
N. Kingstown, RI 02852
Phone: 401-294-2030
Web site: www.innova.com

Irwin Industrial Tools (Vise Grips)
Web site: www.irwin.com

Lincoln Electric Company (welding equipment)
22801 St. Clair Avenue
Cleveland, OH 44117
Phone: 216-481-8100
Web site: www.lincolnelectric.com

Milwaukee Electric Tool Corporation
(electric and cordless power tools)
13135 W. Lisbon Road
Brookfield, WI 53005
Phone: 800-729-3878
Web site: www.milwaukeetool.com

Mittler Bros. Machine and Tool (hydraulic tube benders)
P.O. Box 110
Foristell, MO 63348-0110
1-800-467-2464 (U.S. only)
1-636-745-7757
Web site: www.mittlerbros.com

National Detroit, Inc.
(pneumatic sanding, grinding and buffing tools)
P.O. Box 2285
Rockford, IL 61131
Phone: 815-877-4041
Web site: www.nationaldetroit.com

N.O.S. (nitrous oxide kits and components)
Web site: www.holley.com

P-Ayr Products (foam mock-up engines, transmissions, accessories)
719 Delaware Street
Leavenworth, KS 66048
1-913-651-5543
Sales: 1-800-322-3285
Web site: www.payr.com

PlasmaCAM, Inc. (CNC plasma cutting machines)
P.O. Box 19818
Colorado City, CO 81019
719-676-2700
Web site: www.plasmacam.com

Recaro North America (seats)
Web site: www.recaro-nao.com

Ringers Gloves (work gloves, shoes)
335 Science Drive
Moorpark, CA 93021
1-800-421-8454
Web site: www.ringersgloves.com

Sears Craftsman Tools
(power and hand tools, tool storage, compressors)
Web site: www.sears.com

Sheffield Plastics, Inc. (plastics manufacturer)
119 Salisbury Road
Sheffield, MA 01257
1-916-989-0643
Web site: www.sheffieldplastics.com

Sheffield Platers, Inc. (chrome plating)
9850 Waples Street
San Diego, CA 92121
1-800-227-9242
Web site: www.SheffieldPlaters.com

Special Effect Supply Corp. (vacuum-forming machines)
164 East Center Street
North Salt Lake, UT 84054
Phone: 801-936-9762
Web site: www.fxsupply.com

Sata (automotive painting equipment)
Web site: www.sata.com/usa/

Scotchman Industries
(belt notchers, metal fabrication equipment)
180 E. Hwy 14
P.O. Box 850
Philip, SD 57567
Phone: 800-843-8844
Web site: www.scotchman.com

SEM Products, Inc.
(custom paint and prep products, adhesives)
651 Michael Wylie Dr.
Charlotte, NC 28217
Phone: 704-522-1006
Web site: www.sem.ws

Sharpe Manufacturing Company
(spray gun equipment and accessories)
P.O. Box 1441
Minneapolis, MN 55440
Phone: 800-742-7731
Web site: www.sharpe1.com

Snap-On Tools (automotive tools and tool storage)
Web site: www.snapon.com

Tools USA—Standard Tools and Equipment
(automotive spray booths, automotive tools)
4810 Clover Road
Greensboro, NC 27405
Toll-free phone: 800-451-2425
Web site: www.toolsusa.com

Weiand (superchargers, intake manifolds, air scoops)
Web site: www.holley.com

Appendix II

Glossary—
Customizer's Words,
Terms and Acronyms

A

ABRASIVE WHEEL: A grinding or cutting wheel composed of abrasive grits and a bonding agent to hold the grit together.

ACCELERATOR: Additive to paint to speed the cure of a coating. An additive to polyester resin that reacts with catalyst to speed up polymerization. This additive is required in room temperature cured resins. See promoter.

ACETONE: A ketone group solvent used to dissolve polyester resins. Used to a large extent for cleanup of tools in fiberglass operations.

ACRYLIC: A plastic produced from acrylic acid or a derivative of. Material used in the manufacturing of paint to increase gloss and durability.

ADDITIVE: A chemical added to a paint to improve or create certain specific characteristics. Any number of materials used to modify the properties of polymer resins. Categories of additives include reagents, fillers, viscosity modifiers, pigments and others.

ADHESION PROMOTER: Material used over an O.E.M. or cured insoluble finish to increase the adhesion of the topcoat.

ADHESION: The state in which two surfaces are held together at an interface by forces or interlocking action or both.

AGING: The effect, on materials, of exposure to an environment for an interval of time; the process of exposing materials to an environment for an interval of time.

AIR DRY: The evaporation of solvent in an undercoat or topcoat at room temperature.

AK STEEL: Aluminum-killed steel treated with a strong deoxidizing agent, in this case, aluminum, to reduce oxygen content which prevents the forming of pinholes as the steel solidifies. AK steel has a fine-grain structure and is more stable at high temperatures than non-treated steel.

ALLOY: Metal composed of two or more elements to produce a desired quality in the metal.

ALLOY STEEL: Carbon steel with one or more elements added to produce a desired quality.

ALUMINUM PIGMENT: Small aluminum particles used in paint to reflect light. These flakes vary in size and polish to give a look of glamour and luster.

ANNEAL: To heat metal to a specific temperature followed by controlled cooling to produce a desired quality. Usually to induce softness.

ANSI: American National Standards Institute

ARC WELDING: A welding process using heat produced by an electric arc.

ASPECT RATIO: The ratio of length to diameter of a fiber.

ASTM: American Society for Testing and Materials

ATOMIZE: The breaking-up of paint into fine particles or droplets by a paint gun.

B

BAKE: The process of applying heat to a finish to speed the cure or dry time of the finish.

BARE SUBSTRATE: Any material (steel, aluminum, plastic, etc.) which does not have a coating of paint or primer.

BASECOAT: A highly pigmented color which requires a coating of clear for protection, durability and gloss.

BASECOAT/CLEARCOAT SYSTEM: A two-stage finish consisting of a base color coat and a clear top coat.

BI-DIRECTIONAL: Reinforcing fibers that are arranged in two directions, usually at right angles to each other.

BINDER: A resin-soluble adhesive that secures the random fibers in chopped strand mat or continuous strand roving.

BLEEDING: When soluble dyes or pigments in old finishes or filler are dissolved by solvents in topcoats resulting in discoloration of the final finish.

BLENDING: Method of spray painting in which new finishes or colors overlap existing finishes or colors so slight differences cannot be distinguished. A gradual transition of one color into another as with multicolor flames.

BLISTERING: Effect of pressure from trapped solvent or moisture under a coating causing a swelling or blister in the finish; i.e. water blister. A flaw either between layers of laminate or between the gel coat film and laminate.

BLUSHING: A cloudy appearance of a topcoat that occurs when high humidity is present in the painting environment. When a fast-drying paint such as lacquer is applied, water condenses and becomes trapped in the wet coating. This can be eliminated by use of heat or a slower solvent or retarder.

BODY FILLER: A moldable catalyst-activated polyester-based plastic material used on bare substrate to fill dents in damaged auto body parts.

BOND STRENGTH: The amount of adhesion between bonded surfaces; a measure of the stress required to separate a layer of material from the base to which it is bonded.

BRAZE WELDING: A welding process in which the filler metal has a melting point below that of the base metal. Brass rod with a flux coating is most commonly used with steel.

BRIDGING: Occurrence where a primer or surfacer does not totally fill a sand scratch or imperfection. Not usually apparent in undercoat, however, does show up in topcoat.

BRITTLE: The quality of a paint coating that lacks flexibility.

BUBBLES: Air or solvent trapped in a paint film caused by poor atomization during spraying. Air trapped in body filler caused by excessive agitation.

BUFFING/COMPOUNDING: Using a mild abrasive compound or clay to bring out gloss and/or remove texture in a topcoat. This can be performed by hand or machine.

BURN/BURN THROUGH: Polishing or buffing too hard or long in one spot causing the underlying coat(s) to be revealed.

CAD: Computer-aided design

CAM: Computer-aided machining

CNC: Computer numerical control

CASE HARDENING: A heat-treating process that alters the surface layer of metal to increase its hardness over the core metal.

CASTING: The process of pouring a mixture of resin, fillers and/or fibers into a mold as opposed to building up layers through lamination. This technique produces different physical properties from laminating.

CATALYST: Technically considered an initiator, catalyst is the name given to the chemical added to resin or gel coat to initiate cure. Additive for paint to enhance the curing process.

CELLULOSE: Natural polymer or resin derived from cottonseed oil to make paint coatings.

CHALKING: The result of weathering of a paint film resulting in a white powdery appearance.

CHANNEL: The lowering of a car over the frame by raising the section of the floor that the frame sits on. This requires a whole new floor board in most cases and make a rusty car a perfect candidate for this process in many cases.

CHECKING: Tiny cracks or splitting in the surface of a paint film usually seen in a lacquer. Caused by improper film formation or excessive film build. Sometimes called crow's feet.

CHEMICAL STAIN/SPOTTING: Circular, oblong or irregular spots or discoloration on areas of finish caused by reactive

chemicals mixing with air pollution (coal and high sulfur emissions), acid rain and snow.

CHIPPING: Removal of finish usually due to the impact of rocks and stones.

CHOP: Reducing the height of the top of a car by "chopping" out a section of material from a horizontal section of the roof near the windows area.

CHOPPED STRAND MAT: A fiberglass reinforcement consisting of short strands of fiber arranged in a random pattern and held together with a binder.

CHOPPER: A custom motorcycle with modifications that typically include a raked and stretched frame with an extended fork.

COAT/SINGLE: Application of undercoat or topcoat over the surface using a 75 percent overlap of spray. Overlap recommendation varies between paint types, manufacturers, and painter's technique.

COAT/DOUBLE: Two single coats with longer flash time.

COLORANT: Made with ground pigments, solvent and resin. Used in the intermix system to produce colors.

COLOR COAT: The application of color to a prepared surface.

COLOR MATCH: Two separate applications of paint exhibiting no perceptible difference in color shade or tone when viewed under the same conditions.

COLOR RETENTION: The ability of a color to retain its true shade over an extended period of time. A color that is color fast.

COLOR STANDARD: A small sprayed-out sample of OEM color. This is the established requirement for a given color code. The color the car is supposed to be from the factory.

COMPLEMENTARY COLORS: Colors that are opposite each other on the color wheel.

COMPRESSIVE STRENGTH: The stress a given material can withstand when compressed. Described in ASTM D-695.

CONCENTRATION: The ratio of pigment in paint to resins in paint.

COVERAGE: The ability of a pigmented color to conceal or cover a surface.

CRATERING: The forming of holes in a film due to contamination.

CRAZING: Fine line cracks in the surface of the paint finish. Cracking of gel coat or resin due to stress.

CROSSCOAT: Applying paint in a crisscross pattern. Single coat applied in one direction with a second single coat applied at 90° to the first.

CROW'S FEET: See Checking.

CURE: The chemical reaction of a coating during the drying process, leaving it insoluble.

CURDLING: The gelling or partial cure of paint due to incompatible materials.

CURTAINS: Large sagging or runs of paint due to improper application.

CUT IN: Painting of the edges of parts before installation.

CURE TIME: Time between introduction of catalyst or initiator to a polymer and final cure.

CURING AGENT: A catalytic or reactive agent which when added to a resin causes polymerization; synonymous with hardener.

CYCLE: The complete, repeating sequence of operations in a process or part of a process. In molding, the cycle time is the period (or elapsed time) between a certain point in one cycle and the same point in the next.

D

DEFINED ORIENTATION: The dispersion of metallic or mica flake with a definite pattern.

DELAMINATION: The peeling of a finish having improper adhesion. The separation of composite layers from each other.

DENSITY: A comparison of weight per volume, measured in pounds per cubic foot.

DEPTH: Lighter or darker in comparing two colors. The first adjustment in color matching.

DIE-BACK: The gradual loss of gloss due to continued evaporation of solvent after polishing.

DIMENSIONAL STABILITY: A description of the change in size of an object during the molding process or in varying temperature conditions or under various loads.

DIRECT (FACE): The color viewed from head-on (90 degrees).

DISPERSION LACQUER: Particles of lacquer paint suspended or dispersed in a solvent which is not strong enough for total solution.

DISTORTION: A change in shape from that which is intended.

D.O.I. (DISTINCTNESS OF IMAGE): How clearly a finish reflects an image.

DOUBLE COAT: One single coat of paint followed immediately by another.

DRAFT: The angle of the vertical components of a mold that allows removal of the part.

DRIER: A material used in a paint that enables it to cure.

DRY: The evaporation of solvent from a paint film.

DRY FILM THICKNESS (D.F.T.): The thickness of a paint after it has dried and/or cured. Measured in mils.

DRY SPOT: Area of incomplete surface film on laminated plastics; in laminated glass, an area over which the interlayer and the glass have not become bonded.

DRY SPRAY: The process of applying paint in a lighter or not as wet application.

E

ELASTIC LIMIT: The greatest stress that a material is capable of sustaining without permanent strain remaining upon the complete release of the stress. A material is said to have passed its elastic limit when the load is sufficient to initiate plastic, or non recoverable, deformation.

ELECTROSTATIC PAINT APPLICATION: Process of applying paint by having the surface electrically charged positive or negative and the application equipment on opposite electric charge.

ELONGATION: Standard measure for the amount a sample can stretch as a percentage of original length before it fails or breaks.

ETCH: The process of chemically treating a material with an acid for corrosion resistance and adhesion of a primer, or to remove rust.

ETCHING PRIMER: A primer that contains an acid which etches the substrate as well as applying a primer. To protect against corrosion.

F

FACTORY PACKAGE COLOR (F.P.C.): Car colors that are matched, produced and packaged by paint manufacturers for specific car color codes for use at the refinish level.

FADING: A gradual change of color or gloss in a finish.

FATIGUE: The failure or decay of mechanical properties after repeated applications of stress.

FATIGUE LIFE: The number of cycles of deformation required to bring about failure of the test specimen under a given set of oscillating conditions.

FATIGUE LIMIT: The stress below which a material can be stressed cyclically for an infinite number of times without failure.

FATIGUE STRENGTH: The maximum cyclic stress a material can withstand for a given number of cycles before failure occurs; the residual strength after being subjected to fatigue.

FEATHEREDGE: A sanding process of tapering a broken paint edge to a smooth finish.

FEATHERING: Slang term for blending or slowly moving the edge of one color into a second color.

FEMALE MOLD: A concave mold used to precisely define the convex surface of a molded part.

FIBER ORIENTATION: Fiber alignment in a non-woven or a mat laminate where the majority of fibers are in the same direction, resulting in a higher strength in that direction.

FIBERGLASS: Glass that has been extruded into extremely fine filaments. These filaments vary in diameter, and are measured in microns. Glass filaments are treated with special binders and processed similar to textile fibers. These fibers come in many forms such as roving, woven roving, mat and continuous strands.

FIBERGLASS CLOTH: A fiberglass reinforcement made by weaving strands of glass fiber yarns. Cloth is available in various weights measured in ounces per square yard or kg/m2.

FILLER: Usually an inert organic or inorganic material that is added to plastic, resin or gel coat to vary the property, extend volume, or lower the cost of the article being produced.

FILLET: A rounded filing of the internal angle between two surfaces of a plastic molding.

FILM BUILD: The wet or dry thickness of applied coating measured in mils (also see DRY FILM THICKNESS).

FISH EYE: The effect of surface contamination that causes a circular separation of a paint or gel coat.

FIXTURE: A tool or device used to position and hold a part during forming or fabrication.

FLAKE-OFF: Large pieces of paint or undercoat falling off of substrate; also called delamination.

FLANGE: An extension around the perimeter of a mold or part for the purpose of demolding, stiffening or connecting two components.

FLASH/TIME: The time needed to allow solvents to evaporate from a freshly painted surface before applying another coat or heat.

FLATTENING AGENT: Material used in paint to dull or eliminate gloss.

FLEX AGENT: Material added to paint for additional flexibility, usually used for rubber or plastic flexible parts.

FLOATING: Characteristics of some pigments to separate from solution and migrate to the surface of paint film while still wet.

FLOP (SIDE TONE): The color of a finish when viewed from a side angle, other than direct.

FLOW: The leveling properties of a wet paint film.

FOGCOAT: A final atomized coat of paint, usually applied at higher air pressure and at greater distance than normal to aid in distributing the metallic particles of paint into an even pattern.

FOAM: A lightweight, cellular plastic material containing gas-filled voids. Typical foams include urethane, PVC and polyester.

FOAM-IN-PLACE: The process of creating a foam by the combination of two liquid polymers.

FORCE DRY: Speed of drying due to application of heat.

G

GEL: The irreversible point at which a polymer changes from a liquid to a semi-solid. Sometimes called the "B" stage.

GEL COAT: A surface coat of a specialized polyester resin, either colored or clear, providing a cosmetic enhancement and weatherability to a fiberglass laminate.

GEL TIME: The length of time from catalyzation to gel or "B" stage.

GLAZE: A non-abrasive polishing compound used to gain gloss and shine.

GLOSS: Reflectance of light from a painted surface. Measured at different degrees by instruments known as gloss meters.

GOOD SIDE: The side of a molding in contact with a mold surface.

GREEN: Resin which has not completely cured and is still rather soft and rubbery.

GRAYNESS: The amount of black or white in a specific color.

GRINDING: Operation using a coarse abrasive, usually a spinning disc to remove material such as metal, paint, undercoat, rust, etc.

GROUND COAT: Highly pigmented coat of paint applied before a transparent color to speed hiding.

GUIDE COAT: A mist coat of a different color, usually primer, to aid in getting a panel sanded straight. A dry contrasting color applied to primer prior to sanding. This coat remains in the low areas and imperfections during the sanding process. When removed, imperfections are eliminated.

GUIDE PIN: A pin which guides mold halves into alignment on closing.

H

HAND LAMINATE: The process of manually building up layers of fiberglass and resin using hand rollers, brushes and spray equipment.

HANDSLICK: The time it takes for a wet paint film to become ready for another coat of paint.

HARDENER: A substance or mixture added to a plastic composition to promote or control the curing action.

HARDNESS: Resistance to surface damage.

HEAT SINK: A material that absorbs or transfers heat away from a part.

HIGH BAKE: The baking of a paint above 180 degrees F.

HIGH SOLID: Paints and undercoats which have a higher percentage of pigment and resin (film formers).

HIGH STRENGTH/HIGH CONCENTRATED: The amount of pigment in the volume solid portion is in a higher amount, more pigment vs. resin.

HIGH VOLUME LOW PRESSURE (HVLP): Spray equipment which delivers material at a low pressure of no more than 10 PSI (at the air cap), however, with greater volume of atomized material.

HOLD-OUT (COLOR): The ability of an undercoat to stop or greatly reduce the topcoat from soaking into it.

HUMIDITY: The amount or degree of water vapor, or moisture, in the air measured in percent.

HYDRAULIC PRESS: A press in which the molding force is created by the pressure exerted on a fluid.

HYGROSCOPIC: Capable of absorbing and retaining atmospheric moisture.

I

IMPACT STRENGTH: The ability of a material to withstand shock loading; the work done in fracturing a test specimen in a specified manner under shock loading.

IMPREGNATE: To saturate with resin. The most common application is saturating fiberglass with a catalyzed resin.

INCANDESCENT LIGHT: Light emitted from a burning filament in a glass bulb.

INCREMENT: A gradual increase in quantity.

INFRARED LIGHT: Portion of electromagnetic spectrum just below the visible light range. Can be used to cure paint due to heat being produced.

INNERCOAT ADHESION: The ability of one coat of paint to stick to another coat.

INSERT: A piece of material put into a laminate during or before molding to serve a definite purpose.

INTERMIX: The mixing of specific colors by adding different components or colorants to produce a usable mixture at the paint store or shop level.

INVERTED FORK: Fork assembly in which the larger, lower tubes are on top.

ISOCYANATE/POLYISOCYANATE: Toxic chemical material containing a functional group of nitrogen, carbon and oxygen, used in urethane catalyst and hardener to cross link material into a solid urethane film.

J

JACKSTRAWING: A visual effect of glass fiber turning white in a cured laminate. This usually does not affect the strength of a laminate, but could be an indication of materials incompatibility.

JIG: Any fixture for holding parts in position, while joining them together or to maintain their shape.

JOINT: A line or distinction formed when two panels are connected. Also referred to as a seam.

JOCKEY SHIFTER: The conversion of a standard pedal shift/hand clutch setup to a transmission-mounted lever shift/pedal clutch setup.

L

LACQUER: A type of paint that dries by solvent evaporation which can be redissolved in its own solvent.

LAMINANT: The product of lamination. A composite consisting of a layer or layers of thermoset polymer and fiber reinforcement.

LAMINATE: To place into a mold a series of layers of polymer and reinforcement. The process of applying materials to a mold. To lay up.

LAMINATION: Applying a layer of glass and/or resin to a mold. Also used to describe a single ply of laminate.

LASER: Actually an acronym for light amplification by stimulated emission of radiation.

LAY: In glass fiber, the spacing of the roving bands on the roving package expressed in the number of bands per inch; in filament winding, the orientation of the ribbon with some reference, usually the axis of rotation.

LAYER: A single ply of lay up or laminate.

LAY UP: The act of building up successive layers of polymer and reinforcement. Layers of catalyzed resin and fiberglass or other reinforcements are applied to a mold in order to make a part.

LET DOWN: The process of reducing the intensity of a colorant or mass tone through the addition of white or silver, allowing you to see cast and strength.

LIFTING: The soaking of a solvent into a soluble undercoat causing swelling, then causing the topcoat to wrinkle from underneath.

LOW-BAKE: Baking of a paint film up to 180 degrees F.

LOW-PRESSURE COAT: The process of applying the final coat of paint at a lower air pressure. Used to uniform a finish or blending.

M

MALE MOLD: A convex mold where the concave surface of the part is precisely defined by the mold surface.

MASKING: Process of applying pressure-sensitive tape and paper to a vehicle to prevent paint from being applied where it is not wanted.

MASSTONE: The color of an undiluted colorant.

MASTER (plug)**:** A full-scale representation of the intended part, usually retained as a reference and the part from which production molds are made.

METHYL ETHYL KETONE: Solvent used in many paint reducers and thinners.

METALLIC COLOR: Colors containing various sizes of aluminum flakes. These flakes have reflective properties and when used in combinations and/or amounts, modify the optical characteristics of the color.

METAMERISM: A phenomenon exhibited by two colors that match under one or more light sources, but do not match under all light sources or viewing conditions.

MICA COLOR: Colors containing various sizes and/or colors of mica. Mica flakes have several optical characteristics allowing light to reflect, pass through and absorb. When added to color alone or with metallic flake, cause the color to look different depending on the angle of view.

MIG: Metal inert gas welding

MIL: Relative to paint film thickness is a measurement equal to one-thousandth of an inch, or .0254 millimeter. A typical factory-type paint consisting of an undercoat and topcoat should measure approximately 8 to 10 mils.

MINI BELL: Equipment used for electrostatic paint application consisting of a spinning disk to which paint is applied. The spinning disc is charged electrically and paint is atomized through centrifugal force.

MIST COAT: A thin-sprayed coat to uniform metallic finishes. Also used to blend colors. Sometimes used with light amounts of solvents to uniform finish and/or increase gloss.

MOTTLING: Blotches of metallic or mica particles in a paint film.

MICROBALLOONS: Microscopic bubbles of glass, ceramic or phenolic, used as a filler or to create syntactic foam or putty mixtures.

MICRON: One micron = .001 millimeter = .00003937 inch.

MODULUS OF ELASTICITY: An engineering term used to describe a material's ability to bend without losing its ability to return to its original physical properties.

MOLD: The tool used to fabricate the desired part shape. Also used to describe the process of making a part in a mold.

MOLDING: The process of using a mold to form a part.

MOLD RELEASE: A wax or polymer compound that is applied to the mold surface that acts as a barrier between the mold and the part, thus preventing the part from bonding to the mold.

MOLD SHRINKAGE: The immediate shrinkage which a molded part undergoes when it is removed from a mold and cooled to room temperature; the difference in dimensions, expressed in inches, between a molding and the mold cavity in which it was molded (at normal temperature measurement); the incremental difference between the dimensions of the molding and the mold from which it was made, expressed as a percentage of the dimensions of the mold.

M.S.D.S. (MATERIAL SAFETY DATA SHEET)**:** Contains information and specifications on a chemical or material. M.S.D.S. data on specific chemicals or materials can be obtained from their respective manufactuers.

N

NITRIDING: Hardening process of adding nitrogen to the surface layer of steel.

NITROCELLULOSE: A type of lacquer paint. Also referred to as "straight" lacquer.

ORANGE PEEL: A gel coated or painted finish that is not smooth and is patterned similar to an orange's skin.

PARTING AGENT: See Mold Release

PARTING LINE: The location on a molded product between different segments of the mold used to produce the product.

PATTERN: The initial model for making fiberglass molds. See Plug.

PEENING: Working of metal by hammer blows or shot blasting to increase hardness.

PLASMA: A gas that is heated to a high temperature and becomes ionized, thereby able to penetrate through metal.

PLUG: An industry term for a pattern or model.

POT LIFE: The time during which the catalyzed resin remains liquid or "workable." See Gel Time.

PRIMER-SURFACER: A sandable undercoat formulated to fill minute surface imperfections in preparation for paint.

PUTTY: A thickened mixture of resin made by adding fillers, thixotrophs and reinforcing fibers.

RAKE: The amount, measured in degrees, of the neck tube's angle in relation to the frame.

RELEASE AGENT: A compound used to reduce surface tension or adhesion between a mold and a part.

RESIN: A liquid polymer that, when catalyzed, cures to a solid state.

RIGID FRAME: A motorcycle frame without a pivoting swing arm and rear suspension.

ROCKWELL HARDNESS: A rating scale based on testing the depth of penetration of a specific load into a metal.

RUST: An oxidized iron. Also, iron or iron alloy that has chemically reacted with exposure to oxygen and water.

S

SEALER: Material applied before topcoat to increase color holdout and uniformity of color and adhesion.

SEAM: See Joint.

SECONDARY COLORS: Mixture of two primary colors to produce a second color. Example: red and yellow make orange.

SEEDY: Rough or gritty appearance of paint due to very small insoluble particles.

SHADE: A variation of color. Example 1: a green shade of blue. Example 2: light blue versus dark blue.

SHEAR: An engineering term referring to forces applied to the surface of a given material. The movement between plies of a laminate is referred to as interlaminate shear.

SHEAR EDGE: The cut-off edge of the mold.

SHIP LAP: Method of joining two panels together by means of one panel having a recessed shelf to receive the other panel on top of it leaving a flush surface.

SHRINKAGE: The relative change in dimension between the length measured on the mold when it is cold and the length of the molded object 24 hours after it has been taken out of the mold. Also, the tightening or shrinking of paint film as solvent evaporates.

SIDETONE "FLOP": The color of a finish when viewed from a side angle.

SINGLE STAGE: A one-step paint procedure of applying color, protection and durability in one application. No clear is used.

SIPHON FEED GUN: Any paint gun which uses air flowing over an opening to create a vacuum to draw paint up through a tube to be atomized.

SLAG: Residual metal byproduct of welding processes.

S.M.C.: Sheet-molded compound, usually a polyester-based, fiberglass-reinforced material such as panels of a Corvette body.

SOLIDS: The parts of the paint, pigments and resin that do not evaporate.

SOLID COLOR: Colors that contain no metallic flakes in the pigment portion of paint. These colors have opaque pigmentation or properties in the paint film.

SOLUTION: A homogeneous mixture of two or more dissimilar substances.

SOLVENT CLEANER: Solvent-based cleaning material used to remove contamination from surfaces prior to refinishing.

SOLVENT POP: Blisters in the surface of a film caused by trapment of solvent.

SOFTAIL: A Harley-Davidson frame style in which the swing arm is triangulated to give the appearance of a rigid or hardtail frame.

SPLITTING: The breaking open of an undercoat or topcoat into long cracks resembling the look of a "dry river bottom."

SPOT REPAIR: The process of repairing only a portion of a panel or vehicle.

SPRAY PATTERN: Spray from the paint gun adjusted from a very small, almost round pattern to a wide, flat, somewhat oval shape.

STABILIZER: Special resin-containing solvent used in basecoat color to lower viscosity helping in metallic control and recoat times.

STEM: The component of the fork that mounts into the neck tube of the frame.

STRENGTH OF COLOR: The hiding ability of a pigmented toner or colorant.

STIFFNESS: The relationship of load and deformation; a term often used when the relationship of stress to strain does not conform to the definition of Young's modulus.

STRESS-STRAIN CURVE: Simultaneous readings of load and deformation, converted to stress and strain, are plotted as ordinates and abscissas, respectively, to obtain a stress-strain diagram.

STRESS RELIEVING: Heating metal to a specific temperature and holding it until internal stresses are reduced. Slow cooling required to prevent new residual stresses.

SUICIDE SHIFTER: (see Jockey Shifter)

SWING ARM: The rear suspension fork attached to the frame at a pivot point and by one or two shock absorbers.

SYNTATIC FOAM: A foam made by mixing microspheres with a resin.

T

TACK: Surface stickiness.

TACK COAT: Usually the first light coat of paint that is allowed to set and become sticky before additional coats are applied.

TACK FREE: Time in the drying of a paint film where it is not sticky, but not completely cured.

TACK RAG: A sticky cheesecloth used to remove dust before painting.

TEMPERING: Heating metal to a specific temperature followed by controlled cooling at a rate to reduce stress or to develop strength qualities.

TENSILE ELONGATION: An engineering term referring to the amount of stretch a sample experiences during tensile strain. ASTM D-638.

TENSILE LOAD: A dulling load applied to opposite ends of a given sample.

TENSILE STRENGTH: A measurement of the tensile load a sample can withstand. ASTM D-638.

TEXTURE: The amount of orange peel or roughness in a dried paint film.

THERMAL COEFFICIENT OF EXPANSION: Measures dimensional change of a material when heated or cooled.

THERMAL CONDUCTIVITY: Measures the transfer of heat through a material.

THERMOSPLASTIC PAINT: Material that becomes soft and pliable after the application of heat, returning to solid when cooled; i.e., lacquer.

THERMOSETTING PAINT: Type of paint that becomes hard when heated and thereafter is cured, i.e., enamels, urethanes.

THINNER: Solvent material used to reduce the viscosity of lacquers.

THREE-STAGE SYSTEM: A three-step paint procedure. First a highly pigmented color coat is applied to achieve hiding, referred to as the groundcoat. This groundcoat is then followed by the intermediate coat. The intermediate coat is applied using a transparent mica in a number of single coats until the desired effect is obtained. This finish requires a clearcoat for gloss protection and durability, which is applied last.

TIG: Tungsten inert gas

TINT: A pure toner used for the changing of another color.

TINTING: The act of changing one color by adding another.

TITANIUM DIOXIDE: A commonly used white pigment with high hiding power.

TONERS: Made with ground pigments, solvent and resin. Used in the intermix system to produce colors.

TOP-COAT: The pigmented color portion of the painting process.

TOUGHNESS: The ability of a finish to withstand abrasion, scratches, etc.

TRANSFER-EFFICIENCY: The ratio in a percentage of the amount of paint actually applied to a surface compared to the amount of material used.

TRANSLUCENT: Permits a percentage of light to pass but not optically clear like window glass.

TRIPLE CLAMP: The clamp assembly that holds fork tubes and stem together. Also called "triple tree."

TWO-COMPONENT: A paint material that must have a catalyst or hardener to react.

U

ULTRA VIOLET (UV) LIGHT: The part of the electromagnetic spectrum that can cause fading of paint. Located just beyond the visible part of spectrum.

UNDERCOAT: The coatings below the top color coat that help in adhesion and corrosion resistance.

ULTIMATE TENSILE STRENGTH: The ultimate or final stress sustained by a specimen in a tension test; the stress at moment of rupture.

UNDERCUT: An area of a part or mold that has an acute angle between two surfaces. If a part has an undercut a split mold is necessary.

UNIDIRECTIONAL: Strength lying mainly in one direction.

V

V.O.C. (VOLATILE ORGANIC COMPOUND): Any organic compound that evaporates and subsequently participates in atmospheric photo-chemical reaction; that is, any organic compound other than those that the administrator designates as having negligible photochemical activity.

VISCOSITY: The liquid properties of a material. Resistance to flow.

VISCOSITY CUP: A tool used to meter the viscosity of paint to insure precise reduction.

VIVAK: A thin high-impact plastic that is much cheaper than polycarbonate and can be drilled, cut and formed with heat for special projects. Vivak can be heat-formed at 280 to 320 degrees F. It can also be bonded by Vivak solvent to make three-dimensional shapes.

W

WATERBORNE COATING: A coating containing more than five percent water in its volatile fraction.

WAX: A compound used as a release agent. See Release Agent.

WORK HARDNESS: A condition resulting from cold working of metal.

Y

YIELD STRENGTH: The stress at which a material exhibits a specified limiting deviation from the proportionality of stress to strain; the lowest stress at which a material undergoes plastic deformation. Below this stress, the material is elastic; above it, viscous.

YOUNG'S MODULUS: The ratio of tensile stress to tensile strain below the proportional limit.

About the Author

EDDIE PAUL HAS BEEN CALLED "Hollywood's Best Kept Secret."Ironically, Eddie isn't much of a secret anymore with recent guest appearances on shows such as "Monster Garage." "Monster House," "Monster Games," and "Car and Driver Radio." But for one whose interests and involvement in high technology are so widespread and crucial to several major industries, Eddie is about as down to earth as a guy can get. While most in his position are of the foreign car-driving, suit-wearing variety, Eddie's normal attire consists of a T-shirt and a pair of blue jeans accessorized by a welding helmet and leather gloves. He's been building and riding choppers since he was 15 years old. In fact, his first car was a bike—a 1948 Harley-Davidson "Knucklehead" to be exact. Since that first ride, he's built and owned several high-profile choppers that have graced the pages of all the enthusiast biker publications. While Eddie is, and always will be, a diehard Harley rider, these days you can see him straddling one of his awesome V-8-powered Boss Hoss motorcycles and rumbling down the streets of his hometown of El Segundo, California.

Eddie Paul is a man of many talents, but he modestly refers to himself as an inventor whenever anybody asks him what he does. He opened his first shop, Customs By Eddie Paul, back in the 1970s. This is the business that put Eddie on the map, so to speak. The name Eddie Paul became synonymous with famous cars of film and television as well as wild street customs and choppers. Among the many well-known movie cars that have rolled out of the shop of Customs By Eddie Paul are the street racers of *The Fast and the Furious* and *2Fast 2Furious*, the lethal GTO from *xXx*, the flame-throwing Merc and Greased Lightening Ford from the movie *Grease*, and Sylvester Stallone's Merc in the film *Cobra* to name just a few. A few more? How about the original General Lee from the "Dukes of Hazzard" TV show, the "Mork & Mindy" Jeep, the vans on "B.J. and the Bear," the choppers used in the movie *Mask*, and the morphing yellow Crown Victoria in the 2004 movie *Taxi*.

Today, Customs By Eddie Paul takes in work on a very limited basis, as the shop is now part of a conglomeration of businesses called E.P. Industries, Inc. Eddie's interest in cars and bikes is still highly evident throughout his 25,000-square-foot facility, but the day-to-day business now includes pump manufacturing, tool manufacturing, aerospace machining, prototype development and video production. And as if his plate weren't full enough, he finds a little time to write a book now and then.